Auto Erotica

JONNY TRUNK

A grand tour through classic car brochures
of the 1960s to 1980s

FUEL

Around 1976 or 1977 my dad decided he wanted a new car. Over a few Saturdays, he took me to what seemed like every car dealership in Reigate and Redhill. I didn't mind at all, because I knew that I'd be able to pick up brochures for each model. I could hardly believe they were just sitting there on the side in the showroom, waiting to be taken. My Dinky and Corgi catalogues were well-thumbed and precious, certainly not left out, willy-nilly, on the counter in Reigate Toys & Models. I remember having a brochure for the Morris Marina and one for the tank-like Austin Allegro, both of which had door handles that looked quite Gerry Anderson. We had a very loud Volkswagen Beetle – in the summer, its boiling-hot plastic seats would leave a dimpled impression on your skin so it looked like ruddy orange peel. The brochure probably hadn't mentioned that.

I think of cars in a purely functional way now. At the risk of sounding grizzled, new cars – all with a look of cross impatience – lack the character of cars from my childhood. I can still look at a photograph from the 1960s or 1970s and, chances are, name every car in it. Each had characteristic features: the sad-eyed headlights of a Humber Hawk; the slightly French double rear lights on a Hillman Imp; the half-timbered effect on a Morris Oxford Traveller. A favourite feature on any car was fins on the rear wings. My childhood pal Pete Wiggs and his older brother Steve called them 'Slades', which was a marvellous bit of mental agility, something presumably related to synesthesia – there's no denying the opening riff of 'Gudbuy T'Jane' matched the restrained English flash of a Mark II Austin Cambridge's rear end.

Other people's cars were always fascinating. My sweary Uncle Mick from Dorking was about 5 foot 4 with a comb-over – he tried to make up for this first with loud, coarse language, and second by driving a Mark IV Ford Zephyr, the closest Britain had to a giant-sized American car. The bonnet alone took up half of Norfolk Road. When I grew up, I told a friend of my mum's that I'd like a car like hers – a Ford Anglia. She laughed: 'They stopped making them years ago! You won't be able to get one.' Seeing as I've spent most of my adult life collecting the things I either had and lost, or never had at all as a kid, I'm quite surprised I've never bought myself a vintage Ford Anglia.

But I was fairly spoilt by my mum and dad's run of cars in the 1960s and 1970s. All of them had some quality that allowed me to pretend I was in a TV show: first there was a grey Wolseley (which felt quite *Softly, Softly*), then a royal blue Mini (any sitcom that might have had Sally Geeson at the wheel), a pale blue Toyota Corolla (less exciting but, thanks to the colour, I could imagine myself in *Z Cars*, or in one of the Thundersley Invacars parked around the pitch at Stamford Bridge on *The Big Match*) and then an orange Volkswagen Beetle. I'm sure you can guess what the family called it. Before I turned up, my parents had a Messerschmitt bubble car. Imagine! I had to make do with a Corgi version.

I'm as much use under the bonnet of a car as Una Stubbs in *Summer Holiday* – the joy of cars for me has always been in the way they look. I could easily spend late evenings looking on eBay for car brochures. Jonny Trunk has (once again) saved my bank balance.

**Anglia
a <u>real</u> car for
your money**

INTRODUCTION   JONNY TRUNK

The origins of this book reach back to the mid-1970s and early 1980s when my schoolmate Adrian and I used to go out 'car spotting' – in other words, standing on the pedestrian island of the A325 dual carriageway for hours on end watching the cars whizz past in the hope we would glimpse a rare Porsche, Jag or Dame, or just another DAF to laugh at.

I can't remember how it started, but the combination of geeky facts and model numbers, and that strange collecting bug that young boys find irresistible, were certainly all factors. I had mates who were trainspotters, with that funny little book of train-engine and carriage numbers to tick off. This never appealed to me. But cars – wow! – I loved cars. I'd ask to be taken to London whenever possible, so I could stand outside Harrods all day waiting for supercars to pass or park. This is where I saw my first Countach and, more importantly, my first De Tomaso. I can still see it now, all low and red with a black bonnet.

We went to the annual Motor Shows at Earls Court (1977) and then Birmingham (1978); Adrian's parents had a Granada estate that made me vomit on the Birmingham trip. We'd annoy local garage owners every Saturday by nagging them for new car brochures – and we went bonkers when the new XJS was launched, even getting thrown out of the Jaguar dealership showroom. I'd regularly write to car manufacturers asking for more brochures. We always had to pull over and park if we went past an exotic garage on the way to a National Trust house (yes, my parents dragged me to all of them). And then one day it all stopped. I moved on. It might have been the discovery of John Player Specials, Rothmans and Senior Service that drew it all to a close: my Saturdays were then spent under bridges or in woods, illegally lighting up smokes bought from vending machines. Or it could be that video games overtook my love of cars.

But those car memories run very deep. Decades later I can still spot an old car in the street and know the make, model number and quite often the year of manufacture. When I was looking around for a new graphic book-project to follow *Wrappers Delight* and Sainsbury's *Own Label*, car brochures seemed the right direction. To my amazement, no one has ever compiled a book of them. So I started collecting again. Thankfully the internet, online auctions and the odd specialist shop or dealer give far greater access than those grumpy garage owners from all those years ago.

For the book itself I stuck to a few simple rules. First, the brochures had to come from the 1960s, 1970s or 1980s. A lot of design before that time is a little twee for my taste, and after that a little naff. The brochures also had to be British-printed or issued for the UK market (though I have to admit there are one or two exceptions). You will notice that a lot of the UK brochures feature left-hand drive vehicles – but so did many of the classic TV adverts of the time (watch the Ronnie Corbett Austin Mini advert and you'll see what I mean).

If the car brochures of a certain marque were uninspiring, they would not be included. As a result, there are obvious gaps – for example, Bristol Cars are missing because much as I love them, their brochures are beyond boring. Luckily there is plenty of other beautiful material. When I was growing up, Commer camper vans and Transit vans were ubiquitous, and on a few occasions while I was out collecting I slipped into this world. So we've featured a few of these brochures at the end of the book.

I should point out that this is anything but a completist's book of car brochures. There is not enough space to feature every model by every car manufacturer we've chosen over the period – there are just too many. During my research I met one

dealer who had about 400,000 car brochures stuffed into filing cabinets and stacked boxes, on shelves, scattered over the floor and even in attic space across about eight rooms. And that wasn't counting all the doubles. This really is another vast collectors' world.

I doubt anyone knows just how many car brochures have been printed over the years – different versions for the same cars and ranges, different issues for different countries, large format, small format, expanding pages, single pages, die-cut pages, even flick books. It made me realise just how huge the car market was, and how boring and unimaginative many of the car manufacturers were when it came to selling their expensive wares on paper. This book hopefully represents the more creative, graphically interesting and inspired part of that massive industry. Well, at least I think it does.

Also, I must point out that the reason I called the book *Auto Erotica* was not, as you may think, to allow for the inclusion of a mass of images of scantily clad women draped over cars. In fact, I think it's a myth – if a common one – that car brochures from the 1970s (in particular) regularly used sex as a marketing tool. I found just a handful of brochures featuring women, and even then rarely in a sexual way – more often than not, they were included as really bored passengers. I believe foggy memories of images from other types of 1970s publications may well be getting in the way here. So I chose *Auto Erotica* simply because I think it's a great, attention-grabbing name for a book about cars – and if you ask me, the cars, photography and typography are all pretty sexy. In fact Fuel had to stop me twice from putting the word 'sexy' on the front cover.

While writing the short histories of the marques I realised I'd forgotten about some key motor-car moments of the past: the oil crisis of 1973; the Dagenham sewing-machinist strike of 1968; the DeLorean drug sting of the early 1980s; the assassination of Renault CEO Georges Besse in 1986. Hopefully some of the facts given across the following pages will spark lost memories or trigger new ones.

These days I drive an old and slightly battered 1968 Triumph Herald (with period 'TriumphTune' engine modifications). It's built like a grown up go-kart and has a strange charisma and real personality. It stinks of old leather, oil and petrol. When you drive it everyone looks and points – and some even wind down their window for a chat about 'the old days'. It's not a flashy collector's car but it looks like a little animal, sounds alive and puts a smile on your face – unlike the homogenous monsters of today. Looking at the roads now, I see giant vehicles that are almost indistinguishable, like big black sports shoes (I saw an MG the other day that looked like an Air Jordan). I bet very few of them will still be on the road in six decades' time.

This book looks back to a pre-digital period, when designers had pencils and fashioned car models out of clay. It's a time when car companies took risks and inventors could go a bit mad over a drawing in the sand (see Land Rover, page 113). Engines failed all the time, you needed a jump-start when it got a bit cold and then you had to de-ice the locks and radiator too. There were no electric windows (well hardly), no sat navs, no central locking, no airbags, no power steering, no alarms, no parking cameras, no computer analysis, no dashboard screens, no intermittent wipers, no proper heating. You might have a cigarette lighter, a rev counter and a terrible radio if you were lucky. These were cars you had to drive – and suffer slightly while you were doing it.

I'm not saying it was a better time, but the cars were way, way, more sexy.

3 LITRE MID-ENGINED

AC

AC was incorporated as Auto Carriers Ltd. One of the oldest car manufacturers in the UK, it was established in 1901 in West Norwood. Over the last 120 years the company has changed ownership several times, gone into receivership and produced all manner of vehicles from legendary racing cars to three-wheeler invalid carriages and even a narrow-gauge locomotive for the Southend Pier Railway.

ORTS CAR

Giulia spider
carrozzeria Pininfarina

ALFA ROMEO

Founded 1910 in Milan. Alfa is an acronym of Anonima Lombarda Fabbrica Automobili (Anonymous Lombardy Factory for Cars), highlighting that its founding investors were anonymous. Entrepreneur Nicola Romeo took charge in 1915 and added his name. From 1933 the business was partly state owned. Involved in racing and motorsport from the outset, this innovative company produced some of the most stylish and beautiful cars of the post-war period. By the 1980s the business was suffering production and profit issues, becoming part of the Fiat Alfa Lancia group in 1986.

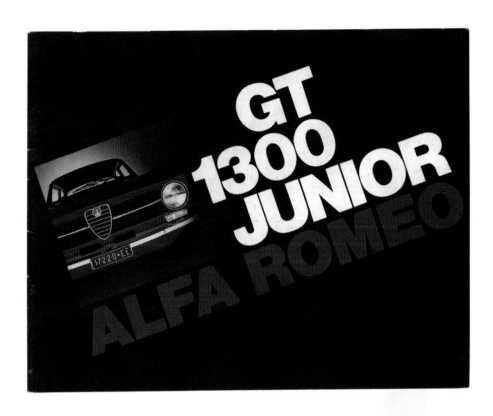

MONTREAL

ENGINE
8-cylinder V-type, 2593 cc (80 ×
64.5). 230 BHP-SAE, 200 BHP-
DIN at 6400 rpm.
4 overhead camshafts.
FUEL SYSTEM - injection.
TRANSMISSION
All-synchromesh 5-speed + rever-
se, floor-mounted gear lever.
Hydraulically-operated clutch.
Limited-slip differential.
**FOUR AIR-COOLED DISC BRA-
KES**, servo-operated with double
circuit. Braking power regulator
on rear wheels.
TYRES 195/70 VR × 14.
DIMENSIONS
Length: 13' 10'' (422 cm). Width:
5' 6'' (167.2 cm). Height: 3' 11.5''
(120.5 cm). Weight: 2926 lbs
(1330 kg).
PERFORMANCE
Maximum speed: more than
220 km/h (136 mph).
Acceleration:
- Standing kilometre in 28.2 s.
- 0-60 mph in 7.6 s.

ALFA ROMEO MONTREAL

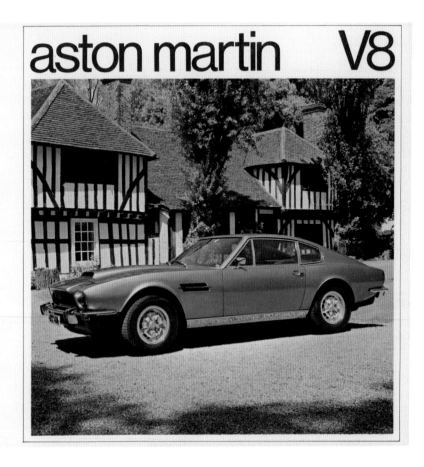

aston martin V8

ASTON MARTIN

An independent British manufacturer of sports cars and grand tour vehicles, Aston Martin was founded in 1913 by Lionel Martin and Robert Bamford, but really shifted into overdrive when it was bought and saved (for the fourth time) in 1947 by engineering specialists David Brown Ltd. Brown also acquired Lagonda and, incidentally, made the gearing for the GPO Tower's revolving restaurant. In 1950 they began manufacturing the Le Mans prototype 'DB' (David Brown) car. The DB5 was driven by Sean Connery as James Bond in the film *Goldfinger* (1964), bringing Aston Martin to a worldwide audience.

With your Amphicar giving you inner harmony and recuperation at every opportunity, you have the lively experience of unbounded joy in life. At ease, and freed from the narrow confines of the road, you are your own captain. At home, you are nearer the water for your harbour is your own garage. The Amphicar is your luxury car for business, sport or travel. Why don't you read the reverse side of this leaflet to get a general idea of the most important technical details of your dream car?

Printed in Germany 4 770/St/120/663

Be
your
own
Captain!

AMPHICAR

AMPHICAR

Designed by Hans Trippel (the man behind the Mercedes gullwing door), the Amphicar was launched in 1961. The car had a Triumph four-cylinder engine, with four wheels and two reversible propellers at the back. A total of 3,878 were made. Current owners meet for annual 'Swim-Ins'.

The new Audi quattro programme.

quattro

BARNETT & SMALL LTD.
WEST STREET
FARNHAM
GU9 7BG
TEL: (0252) 715616 - 714592

Audi

AUDI

A German car manufacturer with complex roots dating back to 1909. The founder, August Horch ('horch' translates as 'listen', and Latin for 'listen' is 'audi'), joined forces with two other manufactures in 1932 to create the Auto Union.

The company was acquired by Volkswagen in the 1960s, and then merged with NSU to form NSU Audi. Classic Audi designs from this period went on to form the basis of VW Polos, Golfs and Passats. See also NSU, page 140.

AUDI NSU

Range for 1973

AUDI NSU

The new 1973 Audi 80 range.

AUTO UNION·DKW

FIRST-in any show

AUSTIN

AUSTIN MOTOR COMPANY

The company was established in 1905 by Herbert Austin, who had already founded and left Wolseley, Britain's biggest car manufacturer. Austin was publicly listed in 1941 and expanded massively during wartime, fulfilling government contracts and even making Lancaster bombers. It was merged with Morris Motors in 1952, (becoming The British Motor Corporation / BMC, and collaborating with designer Donald Healey in the same year, leading to Austin-Healey sports cars. In the late 1950s, with fuel supply under threat as a result of the Suez Crisis, the designer at Morris / Alvis, Alec Issigonis, was recruited to create a small car. The result was the 1959 Mini, a revolutionary vehicle in many ways. BMC launched the car under both the Austin and Morris marques, with the Morris 'Mini' name catching on. In 1966 BMC merged with Jaguar to become British Motor Holdings. In 1968, under government pressure, this company was merged with Leyland and Austin to become British Leyland. The 1970s were bleak for Austin: the Allegro was nicknamed 'Flying Pig', because of its looks and rather questionable performance, and the lacklustre Maxi and dated Princess and Ambassador models rolled slowly out

FOR MORE OF THE OUTSIDE SEE INSIDE.

of the factory. Twenty-one years after the Mini, the Austin Mini Metro was born, briefly reversing the company's fortunes. By the mid-1980s British Leyland had become Rover Group plc and in 1987 the Austin marque disappeared entirely. The rights to the Austin name were sold to British Aerospace, then BMW, MG Rover and beyond. Currently the marque is owned by British engineer John Stubbs. See also Morris, page 134.

THE CAR OF THE CENTURY

ASTOUNDING AUSTIN 1800

The Mini started it all. A revolution in motor car design. It was given a word. "Incredible". A little later the same incredible ideas were taken a little further. And the 1100 was added to the range. The word this time was "Miraculous". Now here is the incredible, miraculous BMC idea sized-up. The Austin 1800. And the word for it: "Astounding"!

LOOK WHAT SPACE IS LIKE

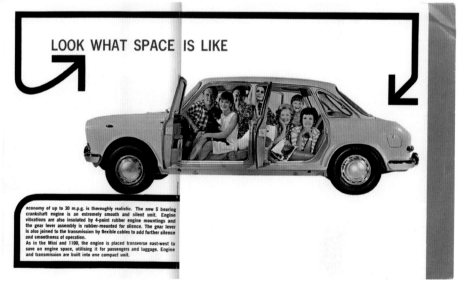

economy of up to 30 m.p.g. is thoroughly realistic. The new 5 bearing crankshaft engine is an extremely smooth and silent unit. Engine vibrations are also insulated by 4-point rubber engine mountings and the gear lever assembly is rubber-mounted for silence. The gear lever is also joined to the transmission by flexible cables to add further silence and smoothness of operation.
As in the Mini and 1100, the engine is placed transverse east-west to save on engine space, utilising it for passengers and luggage. Engine and transmission are built into one compact unit.

another great achievement by **AUSTIN**

The Austin Maxi 1750 & 1500: A good idea made better

Austin 1100, 1300, 1300 GT and countryman

-Still no competition!

MAXI 2

-loads better!

The new Morris Marina, beauty with brains behind it.

The big addition to the Marina range

When you're travelling economy, go first class

Allegro

British Leyland Austin 1100/1300

OUT IN FRONT·
WITH FRONT
WHEEL DRIVE

British Leyland Austin

AUSTIN—HEALEY
SPRITE MARK FOUR

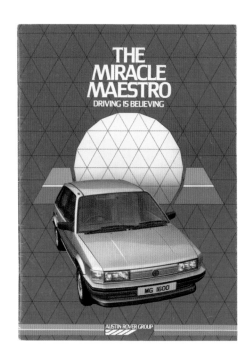

THE
MIRACLE
MAESTRO
DRIVING IS BELIEVING

MG 1600

AUSTIN ROVER GROUP

Austin.
The British People's Car.

BRITISH
LEYLAND

Introducing
the first
Mini Gran Turismo

The fabulous five Minis

MINI MOKE

AUSTIN ROVER

BITTER

This German company, founded by former racing driver
Erich Bitter in 1971, designed and produced a handful of
quirky coupes and sports cars throughout the 1970s and
1980s. The company currently produces luxury versions of
several Opel models.

BMW

Bayerische Flugzeugwerke AG started in 1916 as an aircraft-engine manufacturer, and was renamed Bayerische Motoren Werke AG, aka BMW, in 1922. The company began manufacturing cars in 1928 and survived after the war by making pots, pans and bicycles. Car production resumed in 1952, and after near-collapse and a takeover threat by Daimler-Benz, BMW was saved thanks to private investment from the industrial tycoons Harald and Herbert Quandt. The introduction of the Neue Klasse (New Class) line of 1.5- to 2-litre-engined vehicles heralded the start of the marque's ongoing reputation for manufacturing innovative, luxury and sports-orientated cars. The 5 Series was introduced in 1972, the 3 Series in 1975, the 6 Series in 1976 and the 7 Series in 1978. The first M Series of supercars was also introduced in 1978. BMW bought the Rover Group in 1994, selling most of it off in 2000, but retaining the Mini brand. BMW also acquired Rolls Royce in 1998. The blue and white of the company logo roundel is based on the blue and white of the Bavarian flag.

34   BMW

BMW 1600

BMW 2002

BMW
1602
1802
2002
2002 tii
2002 Cabrio

BMW
2500
2800
3.0 S
3.0 Si

BMW

C · CS · CABRIO

For Performance with Safety and Silence - the *BMW 1800 TI*

unbeatable

BMW 3.0 CSL

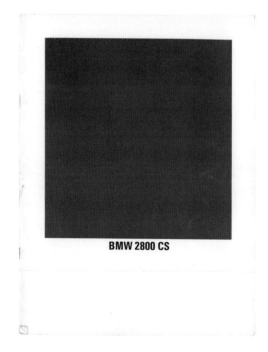

BMW 2800 CS

BOND EQUIPE GT4S 1300

BOND

In 1922 Paul Sharp founded Sharps Commercials Ltd in Preston. In 1949 it began production of a three-wheeled minicar, designed by lightweight-engineering specialist Lawrie Bond. Known as the Bond Minicar, it saw several incarnations and by 1963 the company (now called Bond Cars Ltd) launched the fibreglass Bond Equipe, its first four-door car based on a Triumph Herald chassis. The 875 came next, followed by a company takeover by the Reliant Motor Company Ltd in 1969. The fashionable Bond Bug was launched in 1970, a bright orange three-wheeler with a Reliant engine, created by Tom Karen of Ogle Designs, the man behind the Raleigh Chopper and Marble Run. I always wanted both of those and failed to get either.

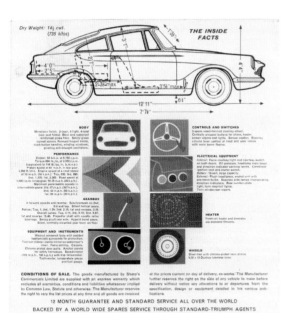

THE INSIDE FACTS

Dry Weight: 14¼ cwt. (735 kilos)

CONDITIONS OF SALE. The goods manufactured by Sharp's Commercials Limited are supplied with an express warranty which excludes all warranties, conditions and liabilities whatsoever implied by Common Law, Statute and otherwise. The Manufacturer reserves the right to vary the list prices at any time and all goods are invoiced at all prices current on day of delivery, ex-works. The Manufacturer further reserves the right on the sale of any vehicle to make before delivery without notice any alterations to or departures from the specification, design or equipment detailed in his various publications.

12 MONTH GUARANTEE AND STANDARD SERVICE ALL OVER THE WORLD
BACKED BY A WORLD WIDE SPARES SERVICE THROUGH STANDARD-TRIUMPH AGENTS

BOND CARS · PRESTON · LANCASHIRE

BOND EQUIPE GT 4S

Built by Bond in association with Standard Triumph and available from Standard Triumph dealers

12 MONTHS GUARANTEE AND STANDARD TRIUMPH SERVICE THROUGHOUT THE U.K.

Write for a complete list of stockists to Bond Cars Ltd., Preston, Lancs. JAMES DID!

BOND EQUIPE GT 4S

Bond Policy is one of continuous improvement. The right to change prices, specifications and equipment, at any time, without notice, is reserved.

IN A CLASS OF ITS OWN Bond Equipe . . . for the man who
leaves ordinary family saloons to other people. A car with
the looks, verve and excitement of a Continental Grand Tourer.
Combining famous Standard-Triumph engineering with
Italian inspired Bond design. Safety with strength—
the modified Herald chassis gives superb road holding,
while inside the Equipe is as comfortable as a limousine.
If you find ordinary cars commonplace, this is the car for you!

for those who find ordinary cars

commonplace

A new motoring experience

new from Chrysler
Simca 1000 Coupe, body by Bertone

CHRYSLER

One of the big three US car manufacturers (alongside General Motors and Ford), the company was founded by Walter Chrylser in 1925. Through cunning brand diversification and acquisitions (including Dodge and Fargo) it grew massively. By the early 1960s it had expanded into Europe, buying controlling shares in Simca, Barreiros and the Rootes Group. British- manufactured cars kept their original names until 1976, when the company eventually retired several classic British marques including Hillman and Sunbeam, renaming them as Chryslers. Simca cars were also branded Chrysler-Simca or just Chrysler outside France. A new partnership with Matra Automobiles began in 1969 to develop sports cars (Matra-Simca). As a result, Chrysler lost interest in Rootes Group products. Confusing rebranding and mismatching of brands followed. In 1978 Chrysler Europe was sold for the token fee of one US dollar to PSA Peugeot Citroën.

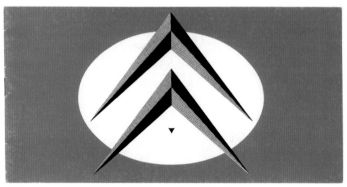

CITROËN

Started in 1919 by French industrialist André-Gustave Citroën, the company was innovative from the beginning, producing groundbreaking cars with groundbreaking technology. In 1934 the Traction Avant (the TA) became the first production car range with independent suspension and front-wheel drive. In 1948 the 2CV or Deux Chevaux (literally two horsepower), was introduced as a bestselling alternative to the horse, with 9 million sold. Then in 1955 the space-age DS was launched (DS sounds like 'goddess'

in French). It was the first production car with disc brakes and high pressure hydraulic suspension – and it had a futuristic look like no other. Ambitious expansion plans began in the 1960s, including taking over Panhard and buying Maserati, but financial difficulties and mechanical failures took hold and Citroën went bankrupt in 1974. In 1976 a new company was created in partnership with Peugeot – PSA Peugeot Citroën.

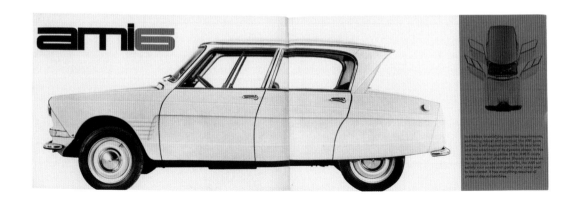

In addition, in satisfying essential requirements, and being natural and practical, the AMI goes further. It will appeal to you with its racy lines and the smartness of its classed shape. In the wax notes of the qualities of the AMI 6 resids in the distinct of qualities. Exactly at ease on the open road and - even traffic, the AMI will satisfy your needs and gratify your every wish to the utmost. It has everything required of present-day automobiles.

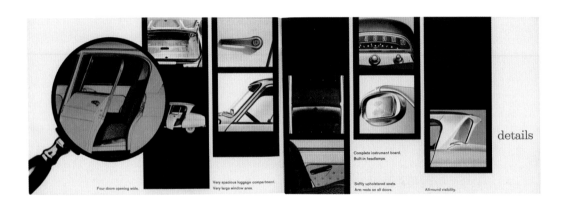

details

Four doors opening wide.

Very spacious luggage compartment.
Very large window area.

Complete instrument board.
Built-in headlamps.

Softly upholstered seats.
Arm rests on all doors.

All-round visibility.

Like all other Citroën cars, the AMI 6 is a
front-wheel drive model. This ensures ideal
road-holding qualities. It has been designed to
cope with all driving conditions. On any type
of road, its adhesion is astonishing, front and
rear; each wheel is independently sprung and
fitted with a system that cuts out all risk of
bouncing even on the roughest surfaces, any
vibrations of the unsprung masses being
absorbed by an inertia-type damper.
With the AMI 6, you will be able to keep up
very high averages in complete safety.

Front-wheel drive

safety first-class road holding

citroën **ami6**

comfort

suspension

Whenever the load, the state of the roads or the length of the journey, the AMI eliminates all fatigue for both driver and passengers. Thanks to the interconnection between front and back wheels, its extremely smooth suspension cuts out oscillation and "pitching".

seats

The two wide and roomy bench seats for four people are covered with an elastic fabric; their shape has been carefully studied to cater for all the positions of the human body when sitting and to give all-round soft support. These seats are very practical since they can be taken out for camping. By removing the rear bench seat, bulky loads can be carried.

ami6

CITROËN

VISA
GSA
CX

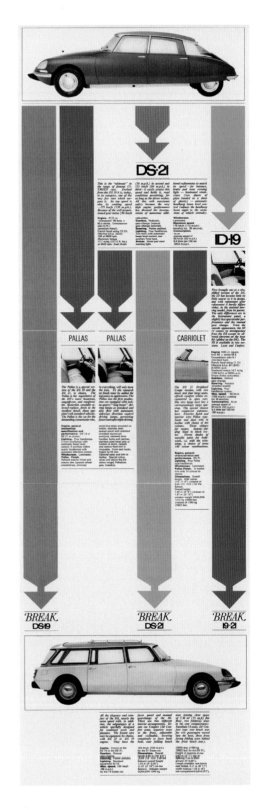

range "d"

in **LENGTH**

miraculously, the 2CV welcomes in **HEIGHT** things no other   car would ever accept.   See how generous she is!

in **WIDTH**

CITROËN VISA

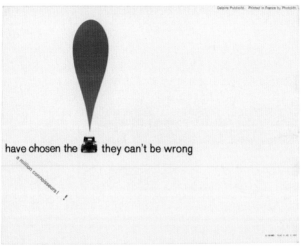

CRAYFORD

A coachbuilding company based in Kent, from the early 1960s Crayford specialised in conversions of coupes into convertibles, even making 57 soft top Wolseley Hornets as prizes for the Heinz 57 competition of 1966. The founders, Jeffrey Smith and David McMullan, were always keen on ATVs (All-Terrain Vehicles) and discovered the Amphicat, made by Beehive Industries in Canada. This was successfully imported by Crayford, as were subsequent models. The Amphicat is a six-wheel drive all-terrain vehicle and yes, The Banana Splits did drive about in them. Sales of these unique buggies across Europe kept the Crayford conversion business alive.

the new
daffodil

fully automatic

DAF

This Dutch truck manufacturer was started in 1928 by Hubert Van Doorne, who was later joined by his brother. In 1932 the company was renamed Van Doorne's Aanhangwagenfabriek (Van Doorne's Trailer Factory), which was shortened to DAF. Car production began in 1958, with the launch of the DAF 600 with its unique 'variomatic' non-step fully-automatic transmission system. The Daffodil was introduced from 1961, with three progressive models, the DAF 30, 31 and 32. The Michelotti-designed 44 followed, and subsequent models 55 and 66 consolidated Volvo's interest in the company. The Swedish company purchased a 33 per cent stake in 1972 and bought it outright in 1975.

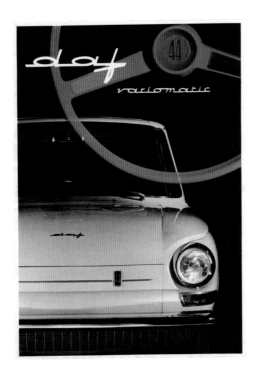

DATSUN

DATSUN ....in the U.K.

DATSUN 180B
Hardtop SSS

DATSUN

The Kaishinsha Motorcar Works built the DAT car in 1914. An acronym of company partners Den, Aoyama and Takeuchi, the name also roughly translates as 'dash off like a frightened rabbit'. DAT Motorcar Co. was established in 1925 and in 1933 started making a small 495cc vehicle to fit in with new government driving laws. The resulting car was called the Datson – literally 'son of Dat'. The name changed to Datsun when the Nissan Group took over later

in the same year. Heavily influenced by Austin (a situation that allegedly came close to lawsuits), the company expanded, eventually sending its own cars worldwide. Datsun cars arrived in the UK in the late 1960s, with impressive sales of their well-priced Cherry and Sunny models from 1972 onwards. Over the following decade Nissan, Datsun's holding company, regularly found themselves at the top of the UK sales charts.

DATSUN 100A

**2-DOOR SALOON
4-DOOR SALOON
ESTATE**

DE TOMASO

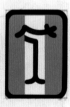

DE TOMASO

An Italian motor company started by the Argentinian racing driver Alejandro de Tomaso in 1959. Established to manufacture racing cars, in the 1960s and 1970s De Tomaso produced a range of charismatic grand tourers and sports cars (including the Pantera) using Ford engines. Acquiring Maserati from Citroën in 1976, the business went into liquidation in 2004. It is currently owned by Ideal Ventures, based in Hong Kong, (China).

Pantera L

Vettura: berlinetta monoscocca.

Motore: 8 cilindri a V di 90°, in posizione posteriore centrale, albero a gomiti su 5 supporti, valvole in testa comandate da albero di distribuzione nel basamento, recupero del gioco automatico. Alesaggio/corsa 101,6x88,9, cilindrata totale 5763 cmc, potenza 300 CV. Olio Agip Sint 2000 SAE 10 W/50.

Cambio: a 5 velocità sincronizzate + retromarcia, differenziale autobloccante. Olio Agip F1 Rotra MP SAE 85 W/90.

Sospensioni: anteriori e posteriori a ruote indipendenti con quadrilateri deformabili ed ammortizzatori idraulici telescopici a doppio effetto coassiali con molle ad elica, barre stabilizzatrici torsionali trasversali.

Freni: a disco sulle 4 ruote con doppio circuito frenante. Olio Agip F1 Brake Fluid Super HD.

Dimensioni: passo 2515, carreggiata anteriore 1450, posteriore 1460, lungh.4270, alt. 1100, posti 2.

Velocità: oltre 260 Km/h.

Accessori standard: aria condizionata, alza cristalli elettrici, fari allo iodio, ruote in lega leggera, bloccasterzo, appoggia-testa, cristalli atermici azzurrati.

De Tomaso preferisce Agip

...GIRO D'ITALIA 1973...

DE TOMASO "Pantera GT 4"

PANTERAGRUPPO4

Vettura: berlinetta monoscocca, con codolini per ruote racing, e roll-bar. Omologata nel gruppo 4 - granturismo speciale, secondo l'annesso J del codice sportivo internazionale.

Motore: 8 cilindri a V di 90°, in posizione posteriore-centrale, albero a gomiti su 5 supporti, 4 carburatori, Weber doppio-corpo, alesaggio/corsa 101,6x88,9, cilindrata totale 5763 cmc., rapporto di compressione 11:1, potenza massima oltre 500 CV a 7000 giri/min. Olio Agip Sint 2000 SAE 10 W/50.

Cambio: a 5 velocità sincronizzate + retromarcia, differenziale autobloccante. Olio Agip F1 Rotra MP SAE 85 W/90.

Sospensioni: anteriori e posteriori a ruote indipendenti con quadrilateri deformabili ed ammortizzatori idraulici telescopici a doppio effetto coassiali con molle ad elica, barre stabilizzatrici torsionali trasversali.

Freni: a disco sulle 4 ruote con doppio circuito frenante. Olio Agip F1 Brake Fluid Super HD.

Dimensioni: passo 2515, lunghezza massima 4270, altezza massima 1100, posti 2, pneumatici Racing da 14".

Prestazioni: velocità massima oltre 300 km/h.

N.B. I dati forniti hanno soltanto valore indicativo.

DELOREAN MOTOR COMPANY (DMC)

Started in 1975 by US engineer and innovative car executive John Zachary DeLorean, the company made just one model – with gullwing doors and an aluminum body. Production started in 1981, at a bespoke plant built on the outskirts of Belfast. By late 1981 the company was in financial difficulty as a result of poor design, bad reviews and low sales. Rescue packages were hampered by a $24 million drug-trafficking charge brought against the company founder through an FBI sting. Although acquitted of all charges, John DeLorean's future was pretty much over. DMC was declared bankrupt in 1982, uncovering additional evidence of an overseas money-laundering operation with Colin Chapman of Lotus. Just 9,000 cars were made – not many considering DeLorean had claimed initial orders of more than 30,000 before the factory had even opened.

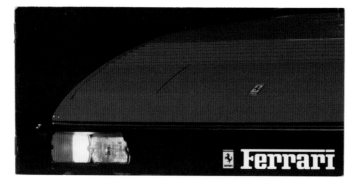

FERRARI

The business was started in 1939 by Enzo Ferrari. With its beginnings in the Alfa Romeo racing division, the company's first badged car was made in 1947. As well as legendary racing cars, Ferrari produced some of the most important road cars ever made. A combination of immaculately designed bodywork (by coachbuilders such as Pininfarina, Zagato and Bertone) and astounding engineering, their legacy remains unrivalled.

Ferrari 330 GTS

365 GTB4 pininfarina

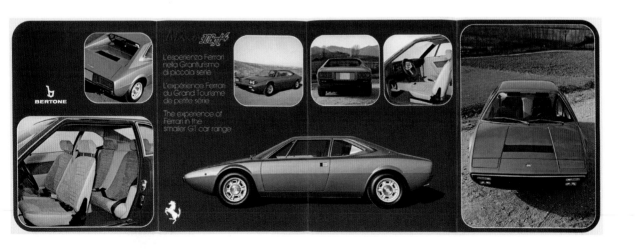

fiat 2300 "de luxe"
with power steering

...GTON MOTORS LTD.
222 NEW CHESTER ROAD
BIRKENHEAD

FIAT

Fabbrica Italiana Automobili Torino was established in 1899 with the first plant opening in 1900. Ten years later FIAT was the largest car manufacturer in Italy. Construction of the Lingotto Factory with a test track on the roof began in 1916 and was completed in 1922. Crisis hit after WWI, but recovery was swift thanks to new utilitarian car production. The Mirafiori plant opened in 1937, consolidating mass production, and the company manufactured military vehicles throughout WWII. The large, functional Fiat 600 with its rear engine (inspired by the Beetle) was produced in 1955 and in 1957 the company introduced the tiny, rear-engine Fiat 500, a car that went on to sell nearly 4 million units. The business expanded rapidly throughout the 1960s

as car ownership in Italy and Europe tripled. 1971 saw the launch of the innovative Fiat 127, but increasing Trades Union conflicts hampered further development. By 1978 Fiat had introduced the RoboGate production line, using robots and automated assembly lines at the Fiat Rivalta factory (as featured in the 'Hand Built By Robots' commercial). The industrial powerhouse grew bigger by acquiring other car brands including Ferrari, Maserati, Lancia and Alfa Romeo. Today it is part of Fiat Chrysler Automobiles / FCA, the world's eighth-largest car manufacturer. Innovation and classic Italian styling have always been at the forefront of the brand.

the **2** versions of the 500

with sun roof

structure and mechanical parts
of the car

Fiat 500

FIAT

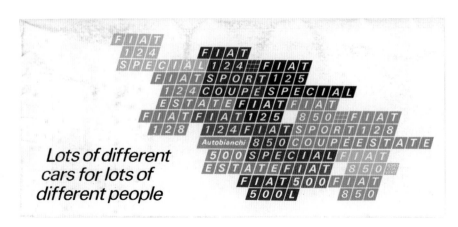

Lots of different cars for lots of different people

The 125 range

High powered luxury saloons
100 m.p.h. 0–50 in 8.1 seconds. 1608 cc. twin-cam engine with silent running camshaft drive belt. 4 servo-assisted disc brakes. Radial tyres. Reclining front seats. Seating for five. Impact-absorbing body. Fully padded interior. Flow-through heating. Variable face-level ventilation. Alternator charging system. Also the 100 b.h.p. Fiat 125 Special with 5-speed gearbox. Iodine quartz headlights and heated rear window.

The fast family cars
Ninety-plus. 0–50 in 9.2 sec. Disc brakes all round. Radial tyres. Impact-absorbing body. Anti-burst doorlocks. Heater. Reclining front seats. Seating for five. Also the super luxury extra powered Fiat 124 Special and the Fiat 124 Estate.

The 124 range

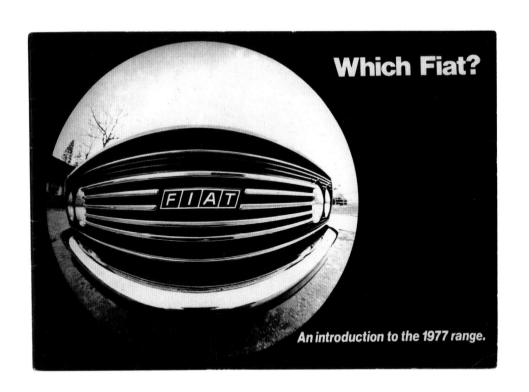

Which Fiat?

An introduction to the 1977 range.

FIAT 1100

Fiat 1100R – An Advanced 1100

1 – New grille and sidelights distinguish the frontal styling; the familiar face of the 1100 in elegant modern form.
2 – The bonnet is hinged at the front—a worthwhile safety feature. The engine compartment can be easily reached.

3 – 620 sq.in. more windscreen area make this an even brighter 1100 with better visibility for all, greater comfort and riding safety.

4 – Wider section tyres ensure greater adhesion. Smaller diameter wheels and a lower centre of gravity mean safety on the road, when cornering and braking.

FIAT 128 RALLY 1300

128

4 new sports cars

128 Sport coupé FIAT

FIAT

FIAT 128 RANGE
SALOON
ESTATE
RALLY
1100/1300SL
SPORT COUPÉ

FIAT 125 SPECIAL

Every day rally versions are becoming more and more popular all over the world

Hundreds of thousands of "rally" cars are produced every year, and their popularity increases all the time. Yet drivers who take part in rallies are comparatively few. So what's the reason?

It lies in the fact that the general public, increasingly knowledgeable about automobile engineering, is finding that it's not in the least necessary to compete in order to own a rally type car. These special versions have advantages for everyone, for all kinds of driving.

The 128 Rally is the first production car of its type made by Fiat. The design is based on the use of a number of technical features which improve the performance and sporting capabilities of production cars.

Fiat 128: protective and protected

Descriptions and illustrations in this catalogue are of an indicative nature only and shall not be held binding. Fiat reserves the right, while preserving the essential characteristics of the models described and illustrated, to introduce at any time and without public announcement, modifications, changes of details, equipment or accessories as considered necessary to improve the models described or for any other reason of a commercial or constructional nature.
FIAT - Press and Publicity - Edition no. 2848 - Printed in Italy - Italy - Torino (xxxxxx)

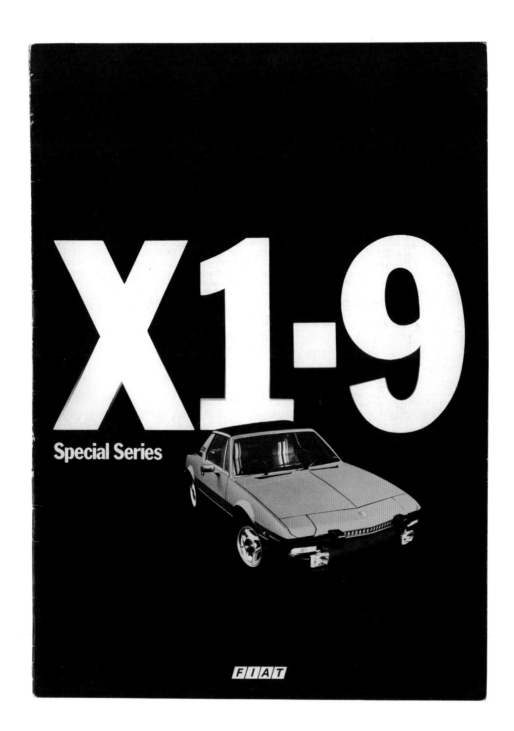

X1·9

Special Series

FIAT

FORD

The company was founded in 1903 by Henry Ford, who pioneered the concept of assembly-line car manufacturing, which matured with the 1908 introduction of the Model T (following the A, B, C, F, K, N, R and S Models). This was the first 'affordable automobile', revolutionising and motorising middle America selling more than 15 million units in the process. Ford purchased Lincoln in 1922 and created the Mercury in 1939 to compete with more luxury brands. The Lifeguard Safety Package was introduced in 1957, offering front-seat safety belts, a padded dash and child safety locks. The Ford Mustang was first shown in 1964, at a World Fair pavilion designed by Disney. Ford began in the UK in 1909 and opened the Dagenham plant in 1931, producing more than 150,000 Model Ys in its first

six years. After manufacturing military vehicles and engines throughout the war years, civilian production began again in earnest with further factories established around the UK. Throughout the 1950s, 1960s and 1970s the UK company introduced a series of bestselling, groundbreaking and brilliantly styled cars that still remain hugely popular. We also mustn't forget the sewing-machinist strike of 1968, when women machinists walked out after a regrading exercise, having been told that their work was 'unskilled'. This landmark labour-relations dispute eventually led to the Equal Pay Act of 1970. Ford ended UK production in 2013. The company is currently the fifth-largest car-maker in the world, and remains under family control.

IRRESISTIBLE

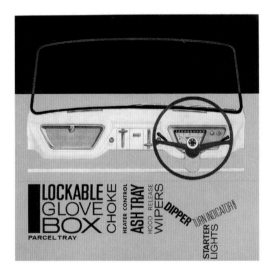

LOCKABLE GLOVE BOX PARCEL TRAY CHOKE HEATER CONTROL ASH TRAY HOOD RELEASE WIPERS DIPPER TURN INDICATOR STARTER LIGHTS

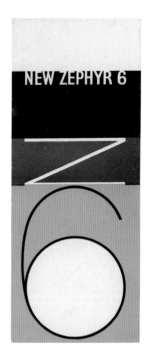

ZEPHYR FROM **FORD**

THE NEW POPULAR

LOWEST PRICED FAMILY CAR...FROM FORD

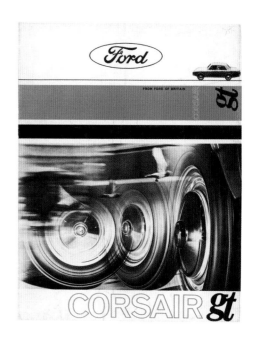

❀ HIGH SPEED PERFORMER FROM FORD ❀ WITH ABOUT-TOWN MANNERS ❀

Colin, quite apart from its performance, the fascination of your Cortina would seem to be its "Q-car" qualities. It looks, and indeed is, a four-five seater saloon little distinguishable from its eleven brothers in the range. I'm very much looking forward to trying it on the road.

The basic shape is identical to that of the better-known Cortinas. We've lowered the suspension, re-arranged the instrument panel, modified the front seats, added a Lotus-green side flash, and have painted the radiator grille black. The car carries both Ford and Lotus badges to show its dual ancestry. The doors, bonnet and boot lid are aluminium, but, of course, that doesn't show.

In the Lotus developed Cortina, the all British-built Ford is reasonably priced, and we have the ideal car for the family or business man who wants to indulge in some serious competition work. This is the car for Saturday morning shopping and Club racing at say Brands Hatch in the afternoon; or it is a properly equipped touring saloon—air cleaner, heater, glove box (illustrated), real saloon car seats and all. This is indeed a Jekyll and Hyde of a car if ever there was one!

Colin Chapman tells me: "As you know I drive pretty fast all the time. There's 105 M.P.H there whenever road and traffic permits. I find it nothing to drive long distances." To this more than modest statement—Colin drives his cars "flat" and safely—I would add that the car holds the road like the proverbial leech—a modern racing car ride in fact—the brakes are all they should be—the front discs are shielded from wet and dust—and the remote control gear change is a delight to operate.

I say with conviction that in this latest product of the mighty resources of Ford at Dagenham and the specialist workshops of Colin Chapman at Cheshunt we have a modern sporting car that is faster than most, as comfortable as any and with inbuilt safety of high degree directly resulting from the lessons learned on the battle-fields of world motor racing. That is the essential niceness of this new car—it is at one and the same time a touring car and a potent competition machine.

What a surprise when the bonnet is lifted—there really filling the space is a twin overhead camshaft power unit of Ford design with Lotus connections and a pedigree look. Like a family car of genteel lineage it will trickle quietly and circumspectly through the 30 miles-an-hour limits and then, in a flash, is a racing car that will perform to the limits of the man at the wheel. The standard engine (as in the car I drove) develops 105 B.H.P., the "special equipment" unit 115. It has been tuned to produce as much as 145 B.H.P.

PERFORMANCE

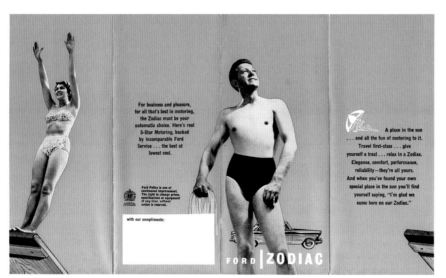

For business and pleasure, for all that's best in motoring, the Zodiac must be your automatic choice. Here's real 5-Star Motoring, backed by incomparable Ford Service . . . the best at lowest cost.

Ford Policy is one of continuous improvement. The right to change prices, specifications or equipment at any time, without notice is reserved.

with our compliments:

A place in the sun . . . and all the fun of motoring to it. Travel first-class . . . give yourself a treat . . . relax in a Zodiac. Elegance, comfort, performance, reliability—they're all yours. And when you've found your own special place in the sun you'll find yourself saying, "I'm glad we came here on our Zodiac."

FORD ZODIAC

FORD ZODIAC

CORTINA

The new Cortina 1600E

THE NEW FORD ESCORT

ESCORT
□ Three door and five door versions available □ 1100 OHV and 1300 OHC engines with single variable venturi carburettor. (Electronic ignition on 1300.) □ Front wheel drive □ Laminated windshield □ Independent suspension front and rear □ Rear fog lamps □ 48.7 cu ft of luggage space with rear seats folded □ Self adjusting clutch □ Illuminated rocker switches and heater controls □ Servo assisted brakes standard on 1300 □ Reversing lamps □ Inertia reel front seat belts.

ESCORT L
□ 1100 OHV, 1300 OHC and 1600 OHC all with single variable venturi carburettor

(electronic ignition on 1300 and 1600) □ Reclining seats trimmed in 'Sandford' fabric □ Two-speed wipers with intermittent wipe □ Side window demister vents □ Warm air available from centre face level vents □ Servo assisted brakes standard on 1300 and 1600 □ Two-tone body side tape stripe □ Heated rear window.

ESCORT GL
□ 1300 and 1600 engines with single variable venturi carburettor with electronic ignition □ Styled road wheels with 155 SR 13 tyres □ Halogen headlamps □ Warning lights for front brake pad wear, low washer fluid, oil, coolant and fuel levels □ Centre console □ Quartz clock □ Ford P21 push button radio □ 'York' fabric trimmed seats

□ Body side protection mouldings □ Four spoke soft feel steering wheel

ESCORT GHIA
□ 1300 OHC and 1600 OHC engines, both with single variable venturi carburettors and electronic ignition □ Reclining seats trimmed in 'Durham' and Crushed Velour fabric □ Headrests with removable pads □ Electronic digital clock with time/date/stopwatch function □ Tilting/sliding screened glass sunroof with louvred screen □ Driver and passenger remote control door mirrors □ Tachometer □ Glovebox with lid lock and light □ Door trim incorporating 'Durham' and Crushed Velour fabric and wood inserts □ Warning lights for front brake pad wear, low washer fluid, oil, coolant and fuel levels.

THE FORD GRANADA

GRANADA L
□ 2.0 litre OHC or 2.3 litre V6 engine □ Electronic breakerless ignition on V6 □ Independent suspension front and rear □ Dual line brakes □ Servo assisted front disc brakes □ Reclining front seats with head restraints □ Laminated windshield □ Halogen headlights □ Ford P21 push button MW/LW radio

GRANADA GL
□ 2.3 litre V6, 2.8 litre V6 or 2.8 litre V6 fuel injection engines (Automatic transmission standard with 2.8 litre V6) □ Power assisted steering □ Gas shock absorbers □ Driver's door mounted remote control mirror □ Tilting/sliding sun roof □ Ford P21 push

button radio with front and rear speakers □ 'Crushed Velour' fabric seat trim □ TRX tyres and sports suspension on 2.8 litre fuel injection models □ Central door and boot locking

GRANADA GHIA
□ 2.3 litre or 2.8 litre fuel injection V6 engines □ Automatic transmission standard on 2.8 litre V6 □ Power assisted steering □ Alloy road wheels □ Tinted glass □ Electrically operated front and rear windows □ Combined radio/stereo cassette (RST 21P) with 2 front and 2 rear speakers □ Electrically operated radio antenna □ Headlamp wash

GRANADA 'S' PACK
Fitted as standard to all Granada models with 2.8 litre F.I. V6 engines
Option at extra cost on other GL and Ghia models
□ Alloy road wheels with Michelin 190/65 HR 390 TRX tubeless tyres on 150 TR 390 FH rims □ Sports suspension including 24mm front anti-roll bar and variable rate rear sprints. Gas shock absorbers □ GLS badge on GL models

GRANADA DIESEL
□ 2.1 litre diesel engine □ Independent suspension front and rear □ Dual line servo assisted brakes □ Radial ply tyres □ Hazard warning lights □ Heated rear window

---

THE FORD CAPRI

CAPRI L
□ 1300 and 1600 engines □ Split squab folding rear seats □ 'Sandford' fabric trim □ Reclining front seats □ Bodyside protection moulding □ Sports steering wheel □ Ford P21 push button radio □ 4 Halogen headlamps □ Louvred grille and front spoiler □ Servo assisted front disc brakes □ Laminated windscreen □ Heated rear window □ Rear fog lamps

CAPRI GL
□ 1600 and 2000 engines □ Tailgate wash/wipe □ Centre console with clock □ Ford P21 push button radio □ 'Windsor' fabric seat trim □ Sports road wheels □ Rear package tray □ Head restraints □ Remote control door mirror □ Passenger door mirror □ Tailgate wash/wipe

CAPRI S
□ Choice of 3 engines – 1600, 2000 or 3000 V6 □ Alloy road wheels □ Overriders □ Rear spoiler □ Tachometer and trip meter □ Head restraints □ 'Carla' fabric trim □ Special bodyside tape-stripe □ Ford P21 push button radio □ Remote control door mirror □ 6" alloy road wheels

CAPRI GHIA
□ 2000 or 3000 V6 engines □ Alloy road wheels □ Tinted glass all round □ Opening rear quarter windows □ Sliding roof with tilting device □ Remote control door mirror □ Luxury 'Verona' fabric trim □ Mono radio/stereo cassette player (RST 21P) □ Special front seats with integral head restraints □ Power steering and automatic transmission on 3000 V6 models □ Headlamp wash

SEE THE NEW CORTINA IN ACTION WITHOUT LEAVING YOUR CHAIR

Capri GT4

The Ford Escort RS 2000.

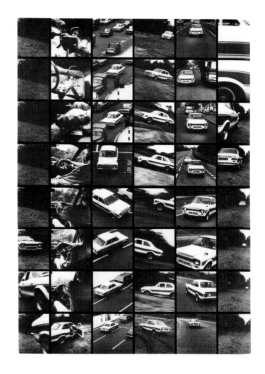

GILBERN

Based in Pontypridd, Glamorgan, Gilbern operated from 1959 to 1973. The company was started by Giles Smith, a former butcher, and Bernard Friese, a German engineer with valuable fibreglass experience. Their cars were available initially only as kits, and later as finished vehicles. They produced three models in all before going bankrupt in 1973. As you would expect, vintage Gilberns have an enthusiastic following and dedicated club.

GILBERN GENIE

HEINKEL

The German aircraft manufacturing company famed for creating bombers for the Luftwaffe were banned from making aircraft after the war. Instead, they turned their engineering knowhow to bicycles, mopeds and microcars. The Kabine bubble car was introduced in 1958.

NEW
HILLMAN
RANGE

SUPER IMP & IMP DE LUXE Mark 2
MINX DE LUXE Saloon
SUPER MINX Saloon & Estate Car

ROOTES PRODUCTS

MEET THE *NEW*
HILLMAN IMP

AN INSPIRATION IN LIGHT CAR DESIGN

A ROOTES PRODUCT

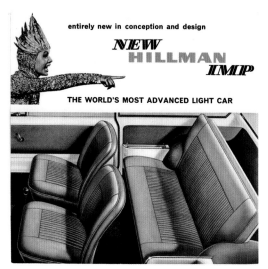

entirely new in conception and design
NEW
HILLMAN IMP

THE WORLD'S MOST ADVANCED LIGHT CAR

HILLMAN

Originally a bicycle manufacturer, Hillman moved into automobiles in 1907. The company fell under the control of the Rootes Group and merged with Humber in 1928. They were a relatively straightforward car manufacturer until 1963 when the Hillman Imp and its fastback brother, the Californian, were introduced. Chrysler assumed control of the Rootes Group in 1967 and chaotic re-badging followed. I still find it confusing, even now.

take a MINX and add ...

economy · comfort · style · safety · reliability

5 top features...all-new **HILLMAN Minx**

HILLMAN ROOTES

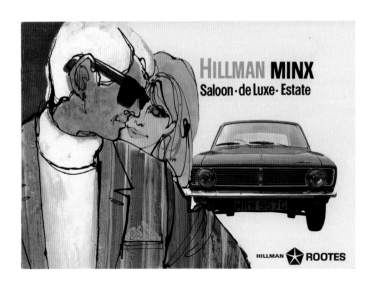

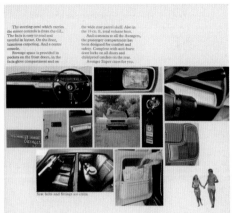

HONDA

Emerging from the rubble of WWII, entrepreneurial mechanic Soichiro Honda began by producing motorised scooters, releasing his first complete motorbike in 1949. The first vehicle completely manufactured by Honda (a small pickup truck) arrived in 1963, swiftly followed by the S500, a sporty roadster, in the same year. It wasn't until the launch of the compact Honda Civic in 1973 that the brand gained international recognition for manufacturing cars, but their reputation never quite reached the same level as for motorbikes. I realise this is a car book – but the Honda Cub series of mopeds (yes, those) have been in constant manufacture since 1958, with over 100 million made.

HAVA HONDA SNOWBALL

AIR CONDITIONING FOR THE NEW HONDA CIVIC 2-DOOR & HATCHBACK

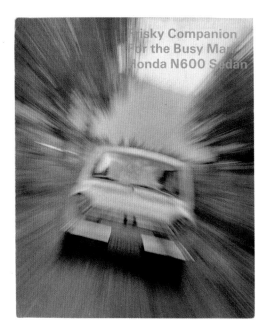

Frisky Companion
For the Busy Man
Honda N600 Sedan

S800

N600 HONDAMATIC

Unique easy action. Three-speed fully automatic transmission, plus overriding manual selection. Designed by Honda Research & Development exclusively for the 'N' series.

N600 STANDARD

N360 STANDARD

ISETTA

Picture shows the
3 – WHEELER
PLUS MODEL

ISA 769

THE WORLD'S CHEAPEST CAR TO BUY AND RUN

Built at Brighton, Sussex

ISO

This Italian-based car-maker started life making fridges.
The Isetta 'bubble car', as it was fondly known, launched
in 1953 and was licensed for production worldwide. The
German BMW version became the bestselling model,
shifting more than 130,000 units by 1962.

JAGUAR

Jaguar was established in 1922 from humble beginnings as the Swallow Sidecar Company, making side cars for motorcycles. One partner, William Walmsley, left to form S.S. Cars Ltd, releasing a sports saloon in 1935 named 'The Jaguar'. Immediately after the war the company name was changed from S.S. to the more distinctive 'British' name of 'Jaguar'. A long series of eye-catching (and record-breaking) sports cars were produced over the following two decades, including the XK120 and Mark VII. The quick and compact Mark II (1959) became popular with police and burglars alike, while the globally iconic E-Type (1961)

was called 'the most beautiful car in the world' by Enzo Ferrari. The supremely successful XJ series, launched in 1968, saw the company through until the 1980s. Jaguar had purchased Daimler in 1950 and in 1965 merged with the large conglomerate BMC to become British Motor Holdings. In 1968 this business was forced by the government to merge with the comedy venture that was British Leyland. Jaguar ping pongs all over the place from then on: I think it's now part of the Jaguar Land Rover group, but I'm really not sure how that happened.

The JAGUAR
Four-Door Saloon Car Range.
XJ 3·4, 4·2 and 5·3

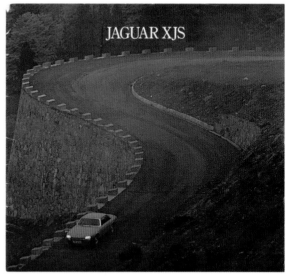

JAGUAR XJS

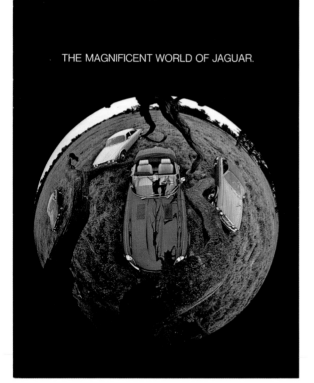

THE MAGNIFICENT WORLD OF JAGUAR.

XJ12C

E-TYPE V-12

JENSEN

The company was started by the Jensen brothers in 1934, taking over and renaming the car body-manufacturer W. J. Smith. Initially making bodies for other car-makers, they released their first car in the mid-1930s. After briefly flirting with commercial trucks, they produced their first sports car, named the Interceptor, in 1952. The 1966 fastback Interceptor we all know and love was created with help from Italian designers. My mate's dad had one, which was cool until he got knifed by a hitchhiker, in about 1977. It was metallic blue. The Jensen car history gets complicated and a bit sad from the late 1960s, until Donald Healey became a director and the Lotus-powered Jensen Healey arrived in 1972 – though sales were still a bit poor. There have been attempts at brand revival, but so far these have all fallen flat.

LAMBORGHINI

The company was founded in 1963 by industrialist Ferruccio Lamborghini to compete with established supercar and sports-car manufacturers. Success was almost instant with the 350 GT, the legendary Miura and its follow-up, the exotic Countach (both designed by Bertone). But trouble hit with the oil crisis of 1973. After going bankrupt in 1978, Lamborghini was revived by the French Mimran brothers in 1984. Sold to the Chrysler Corporation in 1987, the business currently operates under the Audi AG umbrella.

LANCIA BETA COUPÉ

LANCIA

Founded in 1906 by the Fiat rally driver Vincenzo Lancia, the company quickly developed innovative and groundbreaking vehicle technology, alongside a fine racing heritage. After being bought by the Pesenti family in 1956, the company struggled financially and was eventually taken over by Fiat in 1969, clearing a path for several classic new Lancia models over the next decade. Lancia's UK reputation was significantly damaged in the 1980s when the popular Lancia Beta cars were delivered complete with rapid corrosion issues. The original Lancia logo features a flag and lance, because Lancia translates as lance. Of course it does.

LANCIA
FLAMINIA
SPORT 3C *28*

All is new on the new Flavia

Lancia Beta Montecarlo

Lancia Fulvia Coupé "3"

LAND ROVER

In 1947 Maurice Wilks, head designer at Rover, had a slight problem on his farm. He struggled to find spares for his handy farm vehicle – an American Willys Jeep. With the help of his brother and a 'eureka' moment, provided by a drawing in the sand at a nearby Anglesey beach, they set about building a British alternative. The Land Rover was the result, painted in (now distinctive) army-surplus green as that was the only paint available. Showcased at a motorshow in 1948, a new and unexpectedly successful marque was born. The Range Rover, a result of experimenting with larger Land Rover modelling, was launched in 1970. Like its older brother, it proved to be a fine farm tool, as well as a superb basis for utility vehicles. Land Rover remained a part of the Rover company until the formation of Land Rover Limited in 1978. Without going into more confusing detail of ownership changes (including Leyland, BMW, Ford, etc.), it's all currently part of Jaguar Land Rover.

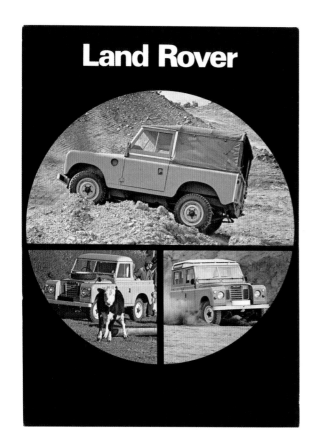

Land Rover

THE WORLD'S MOST VERSATILE VEHICLE

Range Rover

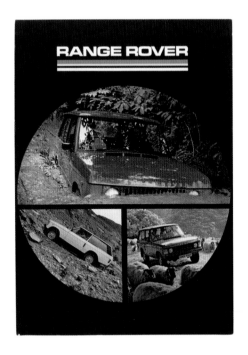

RANGE ROVER

Range Rover

LOTUS

A racing and sports-car manufacturer based in Norfolk, the company was originally established in London in 1958 by Colin Chapman, the daredevil designer and engineering visionary (and one of my heroes). Early cars were available in DIY kit form (beginning in 1957 with the Lotus 7) while the first non-kit productions started in the late 1960s. A series of classic sports cars emerged, but the company had run into financial trouble by 1980 and Chapman found himself heavily embroiled in unravelling financial improprieties at DeLorean. Chapman died in 1982, just before the full DeLorean deception (overseas money laundering) was discovered. Lotus was saved from bankruptcy in 1984 by UK car-auction supremo David Wickins and is now in the hands of Chinese multinational Geely. Chapman never actually revealed the origins of the name Lotus, but he nicknamed his wife 'Lotus Blossom', so the clues are there. Using the same logic, my car company would be called 'Pig'.

éclat

elite

MASERATI

Born in Bologna in 1914, the company's trident logo is based on the one held by Neptune in the fountain in Piazza Maggiore. The Maserati brothers (there were six of them working at the firm) concentrated on making high-performance racing cars, selling their interest in the company by 1937. By 1957 the company had retired from racing-car production and turned its attention to grand tourers. For the next decade, astounding Italian coachwork combined with the road-going Maserati race engine proved to be a potent union. In 1968 Citroën took over, with liquidation coming in 1975 thanks to a global recession and the earlier oil crisis. Saved by De Tomaso (with government help), the company was sold to Fiat in 1993. Then Ferrari. I have no idea who owns it now. But I'd still like one.

MASERATI  GHIBLI

The Amazing Mazda RX-2

MAZDA

Mazda was started in Hiroshima, in 1920. Beginning life as a cork manufacturer, the company moved on to machine tools and the motorised 'Mazda Go' rickshaw in 1931. The business partnered with NSU in the 1960s to successfully develop its own Wankel-style engine (and yes, we all had a snigger at that). As these engines fell out of favour the company adapted, launching modern and successful piston-driven sports and utility vehicles. From 1974 to 2015 Mazda partnered with Ford, and they now enjoy a long-term relationship with Toyota.

MERCEDES-BENZ

The name first appeared in 1901, from the Daimler-Motoren-Gesellschaft (DMG) car company, which had built a new vehicle commissioned by Emil Jellinek (a car salesman and diplomat) named after his daughter, 'Mercedes'. The success of this new Mercedes 35HP vehicle sparked further production. The brand name Mercedes-Benz was first used in 1926, following a merger with Karl Benz and DMG. In the 1930s the 770 model proved popular across Nazi Germany. The company further concentrated its manufacturing on military products and engines throughout the war – with POWs and forced labour making up half the workforce. After the war $12million was paid in reparations to labourers' families. The company grew strongly throughout the 1950s with innovation, style and safety at the forefront of their designs. The 300SL (introduced in 1954) was the fastest production car of its time thanks to a revolutionary fuel-injection system – and don't forget those gullwing doors. Successful exports to the US and global expansion followed. Continuing innovation and iconic design led to the introduction of the 1970s SL (Super Light) and SLC series. In 2018 Mercedes-Benz were the largest seller of premium vehicles in the world – and they probably still are.

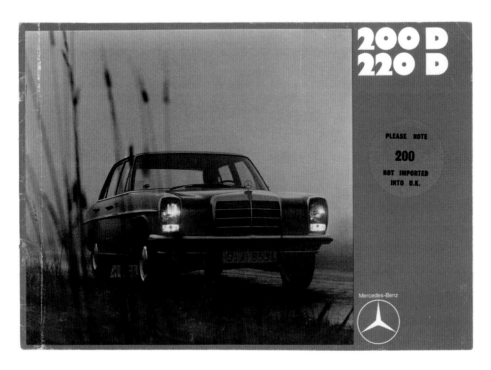

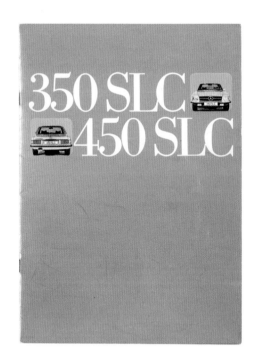

MG

The company was founded by Cecil Kimber at one of William Morris' sales and service garages. In 1921 Kimber was manager for the Oxford branch and started making his own modified versions of the Morris cars, adding 'MG Super Sport' badges to the front. The famous MG Octagon badge became a trademark in 1924 and the MG Car Company was incorporated in 1930. From that point on, the history is complex and quite exhausting, involving the war, Leyland, BMC, Rover – all sorts. MG are now owned by a Chinese automotive giant. But most important are the legendary and classic sports cars they made that we all love, starting in 1936 with the MG T and running all the way to the 1980s with the MG B series.

MORGAN

Henry Morgan, or to give him his full name Henry Frederick Stanley Morgan, was an engineer and entrepreneur who wanted to build his own car. In 1910 he achieved his ambition, producing a three-wheeler with only one seat. He adapted his design to incorporate two seats, which gave it a little more appeal, becoming the first and only car to be displayed in a Harrods window. The company prospered,

beginning to manufacture four-wheeled cars in 1935 (the Morgan 4/4). After the war, the business continued to carefully develop and improve their models, always maintaining a traditional view on styling, engineering and a respect for their original techniques. Morgan have been owned by an Italian investment company since 2019; wood is still used in the production of their cars today.

4/4 4 seater

Cubic Capacity – 97.6 cu. ins. (1,599cc.)
Bore and Stroke – 3.188" x 3.060" (81mm x 77.62mm)
Compression Ratio – 9. 2:1
B.H.P. – 96 at 6,000 rpm.
Torque – 100 lb. ft. , 13.8 mkg. at 3,600 r.p.m
Type of Carburetter – Weber Twin Choke 32/36 downdraught
Number of Cylinders – Four
Firing Order – 1, 2, 4, 3.
Oil Capacity – 7.5 pints (4.25 l.) 1.7 pints(8.1) refill
Petrol Capacity – 10 gallons, 45.5 litres.

The 4/4 4 seater combines the sporting performance of
the 2 seater with the advantages of a family car. There
is plenty of leg and headroom in the back seat when the
weatherproof hood is raised. A fresh air heater for cold
wintry mornings and opening side windows for all four
passengers.

MORGAN 4/4 *performance data*

Cubic Capacity – 97.6 cu. ins. (1,599cc.)
Bore and Stroke – 3.188" x 3.060" (81mm x 77.62mm)
Compression Ratio – 9.2:1
B.H.P. – 96 at 6,000 r.p.m.
Torque – 100lb.ft. , 13.8mkg. at 3,600 r.p.m.
Type of Carburetter – Weber Twin Choke 32/36 downdraught
Number of Cylinders – Four
Firing Order – 1, 2, 4, 3.
Oil Capacity – 7.5 pints (4.25 l.) , 7 pints(4.1) refill
Petrol Capacity – 8½ gallons, 39 litres.

The Morgan 4/4 1600, a true sports car. Sure-footed control, powerful brakes. 4-speed synchro box, remote gear change, full weather
protection. The 4/4 1600 is lively, safe and will outperform all other
cars at the price. The crossflow engine of the 1600 range delivers
flexible power and with an all-up weight of 14¾ cwts. ,740 Kg. gives
the 2 seater lively acceleration. This model embodies a mild stage
of tune. Sorry there's a bit of a queue to buy one – better get your name
down at your dealers now.

131

Morgan 4/4

1600 tourer 2-seater and 4-seater

The Morgan 4/4 1600; a true sports car—some say the only sports car made today. Sure-footed control, powerful brakes. 4-speed synchro box, remote gear change, full weather protection. It's lively and safe. In competition form the 4/4 1600 will outperform all other cars at the price, and the 4-seater is unique these days in that we have really made enough room for them in an open sports car. Sorry there's a bit of a queue to buy one—better get your name down at your dealers now.

Morgan make them like they used to.

Morgan +8

Once in a lifetime a dream comes true. You wish for a sports car that is strong and steady; responsive yet docile; fast and safe. Once in a lifetime that dream comes true—and the new Morgan Plus 8 could be it.
This latest Morgan personality blends with yours—a man in charge, exciting, safe—off to enjoy an entirely new experience.

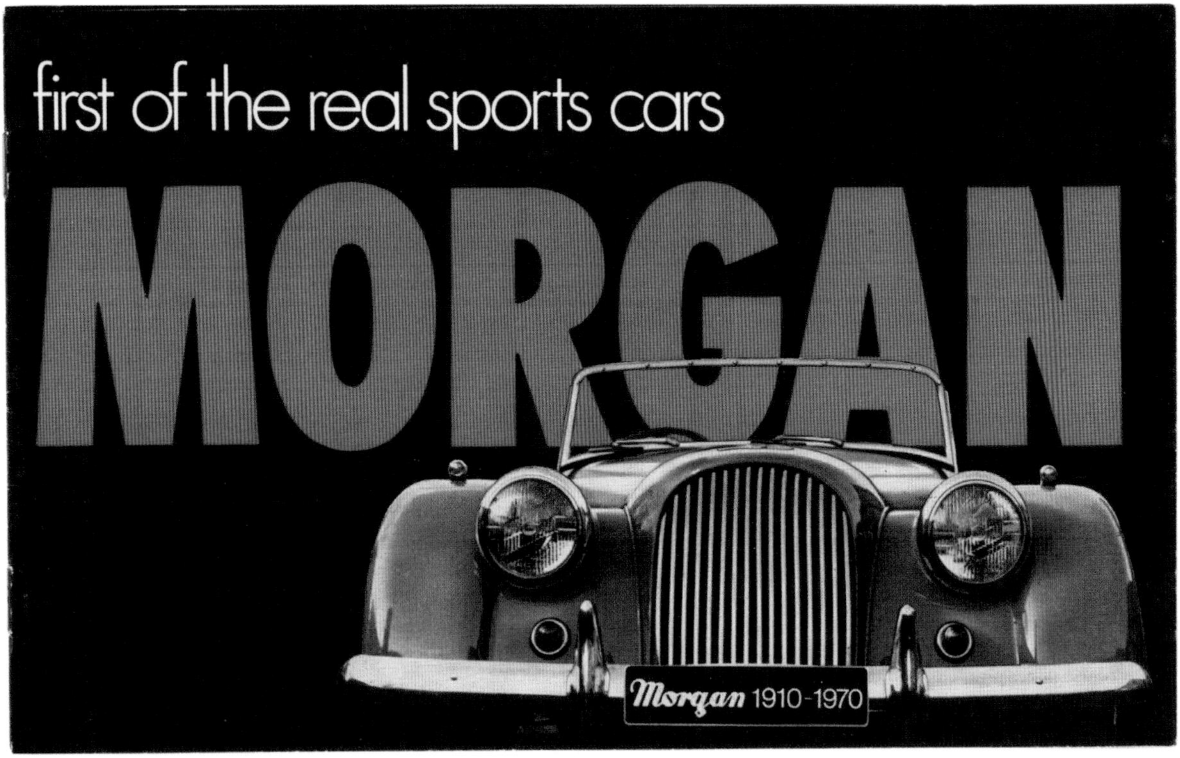

first of the real sports cars

MORGAN

Morgan 1910-1970

meet the **MORRIS** family
..... they're BRITISH, and proud of it!

MORRIS

William Morris began in business in 1892, when as an apprentice bicycle-repair boy, he opened his own shop after his employer refused to give him a pay rise. By 1902 he was working on motorcycles; by 1912 he'd designed a car. Importing parts from the US he would build the vehicles at a disused military training ground in Cowley, Oxford. Employing Henry Ford's techniques of mass production, he expanded rapidly, progressing from 400 cars in 1919 to 45,000 in 1925. The business merged with the Austin Motor Company in 1952, but the Morris name remained in use until 1982, when British Leyland came along and messed it all up by having no real manufacturing focus, confusing and questionable marketing ideas, and hopeless modern concepts that would never make it past prototype stage. They made some classic cars up until then though. See Austin, page 23.

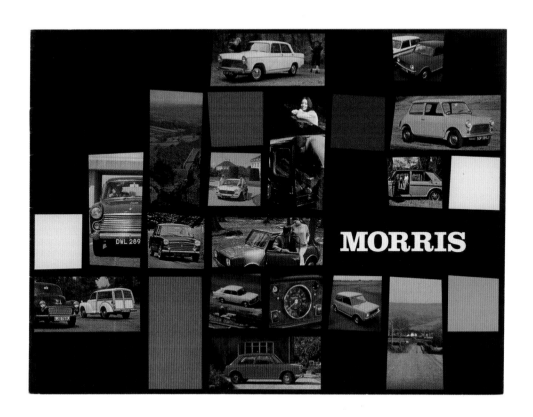

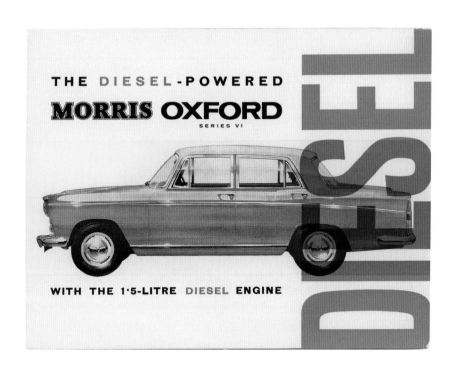

MORRIS 1300 GT.
The one GT that just had to be

MORRIS
MINI-COOPER
AND
MINI-COOPER 'S'
WITH
HYDROLASTIC SUSPENSION

Suspension to match their performance!

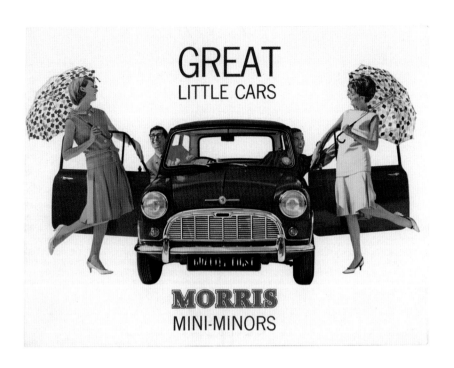

NSU

This German manufacturer of knitting machines, formed in 1873, moved into the manufacture of penny-farthings (with the Germania) in 1886, motorcycles in 1901 and produced its first car in 1905. But the high-volume car factory had failed by 1935. During WWII they produced the Kettenkrad, a lively half-tracked motorcycle. Global motorbike success followed after the war and car manufacturing was picked up again in 1957 with the NSU Prinz. In 1964 they introduced the world's first Wankel engine (the Wankel-Spider, designed by Felix Wankel) – a lightweight rotary engine with fewer moving parts than the classic, piston-driven, internal-combustion engine. But development proved expensive and difficult, and while the models were popular, all-too-frequent mechanical problems damaged the company's reputation. In 1969 the company was taken over by Volkswagen and merged with Auto Union. See Audi, page 21.

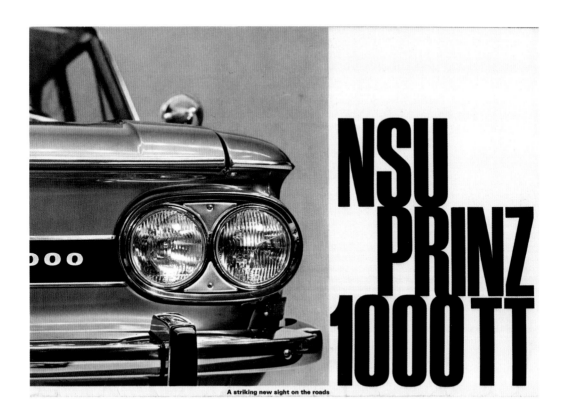

NSU PRINZ 1000 TT

A striking new sight on the roads

OPEL

The company roots can be traced back to 1862 with Adam Opel's sewing-machine business. Based in Rüsselsheim am Main, production was transferred to bicycles and then cars in 1899. By 1931 General Motors had bought the company outright and by 1935 Opel was the first German car manufacturer to produce more than 100,000 cars a year. During the war, nearly 50 per cent of buildings in Rüsselsheim were destroyed, but by 1946 the Opel factory had been rebuilt and was making fridges for the US

company Frigidaire. When car manufacturing resumed, designs were heavily influenced by American styling, leading to the production of some very successful and distinctive-looking models. By the mid-1970s GMs' two European companies – Opel and Vauxhall – were confusingly rationalised, with the Opel brand coming out on top. Opel is currently in the hands of Dutch car giant Stellantis N.V.

the Kadett with the city tailgate

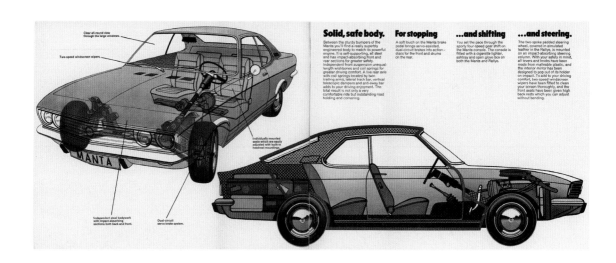

Solid, safe body.

Between the sturdy bumpers of the Manta you'll find a really superbly engineered body to match its powerful engine. It is self-supporting, all steel and has impact-absorbing front and rear sections for greater safety. Independent front suspension unequal-length wishbones and coil springs for greater driving comfort. A live rear axle with coil springs located by twin trailing arms, lateral track bar, vertical telescopic dampers and anti-sway bar adds to your driving enjoyment. The total result is not only a very comfortable ride but outstanding road holding and cornering.

For stopping

A soft touch on the Manta brake pedal brings servo-assisted, dual-circuit brakes into action - discs for the front and drums on the rear.

...and shifting

You set the pace through the sporty four-speed gear shift on the Manta console. The console is fitted with a cigarette lighter, ashtray and open glove box on both the Manta and Rallye.

...and steering.

The two-spoke padded steering wheel, covered in simulated leather in the Rallye, is mounted on an impact-absorbing steering column. With your safety in mind, all levers and knobs have been made from malleable plastic, and the interior mirror has been designed to pop out of its holder on impact. To add to your driving comfort, two-speed windscreen wipers have been fitted to clean your screen thoroughly, and the front seats have been given high back rests which you can adjust without bending.

OPEL GT SPORTS COUPE

"It's a new Opel. It's a Manta."

PEUGEOT

The Peugeot family from Franche-Comté started a steel foundry in 1810, graduating to saw-blade manufacture, then coffee grinders, pepper grinders (we've got one in our kitchen) and in 1880, bicycles. The original lion logo was used to highlight the speed and fierce strength of their blades. Their first steam-powered car was made in 1889. Steam was soon abandoned, but car manufacturing was not. By 1899 Peugeot were making a quarter of the cars in France and by 1903 one half. A mixture of clever design, inspired designers (including Bugatti) and racing guts kept Peugeot out in front. After WWII the company excelled not just in motor-car production, but also in rally performances. By the late 1950s they'd started selling cars in the US, and by 1962 the Peugeot 403 (introduced in 1955) had sold more than a million models. With the design skills of Pininfarina, the models of the 1960s and 1970s (such as the 504) proved an enduring success. In 1974 the company bought a 30 per cent share of Citroën, taking over completely by 1975 to become PSA. The early 1980s saw the rise of the 'superminis' and 'hot hatches', with the 205 selling in excess of 50,000 a year. To be honest, I'm not that interested in what happened from then on. But a merger of PSA and the monster that is FCA (Fiat Chrysler Autos) has recently taken place. The new, combined even bigger monster, is called Stellantis N.V., and is 'host' to fourteen giant and classic brands.

PEUGEOT

304

PEUGEOT

204 PEUGEOT

elegant line,
balanced design

PORSCHE

Dr Ferdinand Porsche established his vehicle design and consultancy firm called 'Dr. Ing h.c.F. Porsche' in 1931. One of his first commissions was from the German government, which appointed him to build a 'car for the people'. I think we all know the rest. Porsche went on to design several tanks for the German military machine and in 1945 was arrested for war crimes. Although he was jailed for 20 months, he was never tried. His son Ferry Porsche took the reins, and after searching in vain for an existing car he liked, he decided to design his own. He created what was to become the 356 and by the time his father returned to the fold it had already become the first Porsche production car, complete with the unmistakable shape that Porsche is still known for. The rest is really motor-racing history, but you might be interested to know that the Porsche model numbering system for the 900 series starts at 910 and not 901 because it would have infringed the trademarked 'x0x' numbering system already in use by Peugeot.

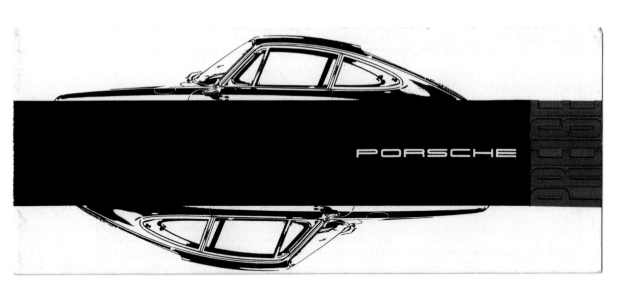

RELIANT Sheer logic

Sheer logic
4 different
ways

There are four Reliant 3-wheelers.
The Regal 3 30 saloon, the Regal 21E
Saloon—the luxury version, the
Supervan 111, and the Supervan 11E,
luxury version. Between them, they
make up a remarkably versatile range.
You may want a fully equipped
luxury car, or a sensible, robust,
hard-working load-carrier, or any of
the half-way houses between the two.
With the Reliant, you get a good
looking, and above all rival answer
to your problem.

RELIANT

The British car manufacturer from Tamworth was formed in 1935 by two ex-Raleigh bicycle engineers, who wanted to continue three-wheel car production after Raleigh stopped in 1934. Over the next six decades Reliant produced a number of classic three-wheeled vehicles, utilising the potential of lightweight fibreglass from the 1950s onwards.

In the 1970s Reliant was the largest manufacturer of fibreglass in Europe and the second biggest car manufacturer in the UK, behind Leyland. Interest in Reliant products fizzled out slowly, revivals failed and the company was finally closed in 2002. On the site of the old factory there is now a housing estate named Scimitar Park.

Load-swallower

Scimitar GTE

Scimitar GTE
High performance estate

The Reliant Motor Company Limited, Tamworth, Staffs, England Telephone: Tamworth 4151 STD 0827

The smart economy car designed specially for the needs of the modern family

RELIANT REBEL

Pocket money motoring for 1966

Reliant make economy make sense with the Rebel

SCIMITAR GT

RENAULT

The French car-making giant was established in 1899 by the three Renault brothers. After several prototypes, their first cars and motors started selling quickly and by 1905 they were supplying fleets of taxis and military vehicles. Through engineering innovation and good racing publicity, the company quickly grew very large. During WWII Renault refused to make tanks for the German army, even though it had taken control of their factories. Instead, trucks were produced by the largest self-sufficient plant, at Seguin Island on the Seine. The site was bombed several times by the Allies, but it reopened a few weeks after the Liberation of Paris. For the next three decades Renault flourished, despite experiencing regular militant labour issues. A stable of classic and iconic models were produced: the Renault 4 from 1966, selling 8 million models; the economic Renault 5 from 1972, selling 5.5 million (brilliantly anticipating the 1973 energy crisis) – and I could go on, but I won't. Expansion continued on a global level, including a partnership with the American Motors Corporation. In 1985 Georges Besse became the man in charge, only to be assassinated in 1986 outside his home in Paris by members of the anarchist movement Action Directe. He'd recently laid off 21,000 workers. The company is now in public hands, with the French state owning 15 per cent.

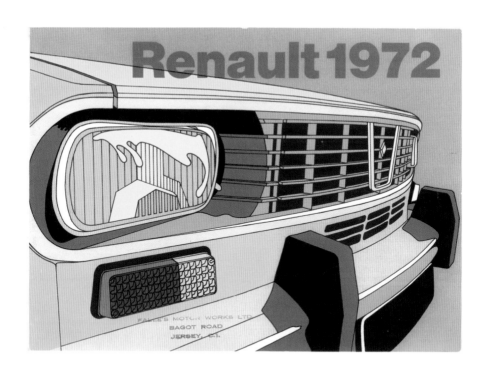

RENAULT
RENAULT
10
8
8S

The 1975 Renault Range

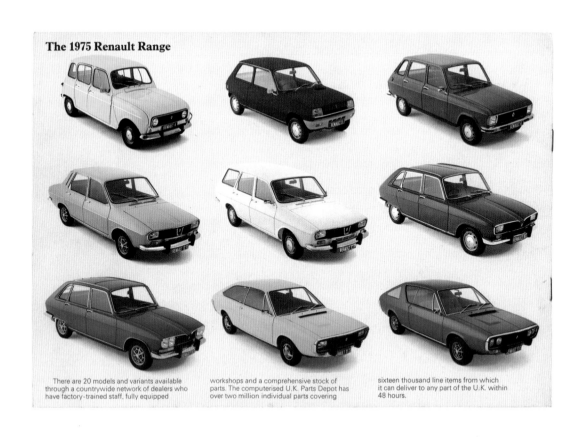

There are 20 models and variants available through a countrywide network of dealers who have factory-trained staff, fully equipped

workshops and a comprehensive stock of parts. The computerised U.K. Parts Depot has over two million individual parts covering

sixteen thousand line items from which it can deliver to any part of the U.K. within 48 hours.

RENAULT 80

THE SUBSTANCE OF A SHADOW

ROLLS-ROYCE

The luxury car manufacturer was established in Manchester in 1904 as a partnership between Charles Rolls (pioneering car dealer, aviator and balloonist) and Henry Royce (engineer). Their first car, the Silver Shadow, appeared in 1906 but tragically Charles Rolls died in 1910, the first Briton to be killed in a powered aeronautical accident. In 1914, at the government's request, the company began manufacture of the Rolls-Royce aeronautic engine. In 1931 they acquired sports-car maker Bentley and in 1959 they bought coachbuilders H. J. Mulliner. Over the decades the company has been responsible for a long series of astoundingly beautiful and extraordinarily luxurious vehicles (many featuring bespoke fittings, for famous clients). Financial problems concerning aero-engine contracts hit the business hard and it was bought by the government in 1971. It has been a public limited company since 1987.

THE WHOLE IS GREATER THAN THE SUM OF THE PARTS

The Silver Shadow is not the biggest car in the world. Nor is it the fastest; though it can show a clean pair of heels to most 'sports' cars. It is not the trendiest: innovation for the sake of innovation is not encouraged by Rolls-Royce Motors. It is not even the most expensive car in the world.

And although the jigsaw that builds up into a Silver Shadow does have many unique features, on the surface a lot of the pieces are similar to those of other quite ordinary cars. A rugged steel monocoque body, a V-8 engine, automatic transmission, independent suspension, disc brakes, and so on. What makes the difference is the detail of the design of the 80,000 individual parts (the average car makes do with about 12,000), the materials they are made of, the fine tolerances they are made to, their finish, their precise relationship one to another.

The first time you set eyes on a Silver Shadow, you begin to see what the Rolls-Royce Motors approach to motor engineering is all about. The car looks right. Its line is clean and timeless. It is relaxed and elegant yet full of power and purpose. In a word, this Silver Shadow has *breeding*—and it shows.

Endless thought, care and testing have been lavished on each detail, right down to the individual nuts and bolts—and this shows, too. Nothing has been skimped. Nothing has been done the easy, quick way when longer, more painstaking methods will produce better results. No expense

has been spared. Equally, there is no waste: you will not find meaningless embellishments on the Silver Shadow.

For example: many cars have headlamp rims; but the Silver Shadow's are individually hand beaten and polished to perfection. All cars are painted; before the colour coats are applied, the Silver Shadow is rinsed with de-mineralised water to prevent streaks that would mar its beauty. Down in the engine, cylinder-head studs are waisted—a feature found elsewhere on aero-engines. In the brake system, hydraulic lock is prevented by slightly 'barrelling' valves—by 0.005 mm (2/10,000th inch)! These are details you might not notice. But you certainly would note, with pleasure that every time you close an ashtray after use, it automatically empties itself into a bin below.

But refinement is still possible and goes on all the time. Since the Silver Shadow was launched, over 2000 alterations have been made to its specification, with each significant change tested over 80,000km (50,000 miles) in France where roads are less crowded than in Britain—and where some very rough ones can still be found.

Someone once remarked: *'There is nothing in the world that cannot be made just a little cheaper—and just a little worse.'* In an age dominated by this shabby philosophy, the Silver Shadow continues serenely on its way rewarding both its owner and its maker. Here, if you seek it, is living proof that Gresham's Law is wrong. The bad does *not* necessarily drive out the good.

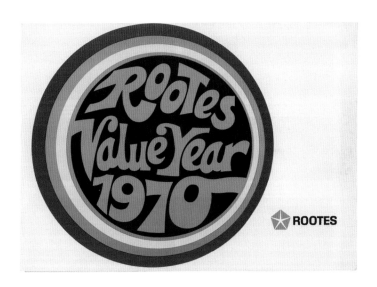

ROOTES GROUP

The company was founded in 1913 in Kent, by William Rootes as a car-sales agency. By 1924 it was the largest distributor of cars and trucks in the UK. Attention was focused on car manufacturing from 1928, with the purchase of Hillman, Humber and Commercial Cars Ltd (Commer). Further acquisitions over the next decade included Sunbeam and Clement Talbot. Several memorable cars were launched in the post-war period, including the Hillman Minx range, the Hillman Hunter, the Sunbeam Alpine and the Sunbeam Tiger. By 1964 Chrysler owned 30 per cent of the group, an amount that increased as the Rootes Group started to falter. Supply-chain problems and the expensive unreliability issues of the charismatic Hillman Imp began to impact on the company. By 1967 Chrysler had taken full control, eventually creating Chrysler Europe. The Rootes name had completely disappeared by 1971.

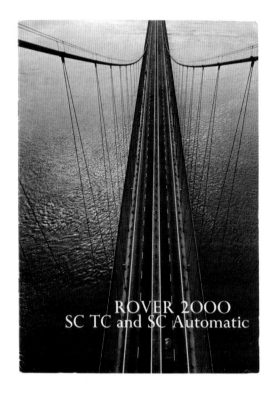

ROVER 2000
SC TC and SC Automatic

ROVER

Launched in 1878, the Rover Company produced the Rover Safety Bicycle, seen by many as the forerunner of the modern-day bicycle (it had two matching-sized wheels and was chain driven). They prototyped an electric car in 1888 and moved into motorcycle production in 1902. Their first car, the Rover 8, was launched in 1904. After a fairly turbulent 1920s and early 1930s the company decided to concentrate on high-quality cars. Throughout WWII they were heavily involved with the manufacture of jet- and gas-turbine engines. By the 1950s (and with the launch of the Land Rover, which eventually became a company in its own right, see page 113), Rover were thriving. Further classic motor cars were developed over the next decade, including the P5 and P6 saloons – beloved of MPs, diplomats, the police and Annie Walker from *Coronation Street*. In 1967 Rover became part of British Leyland – and from there things travelled in the wrong direction. In 1977 the strangely charismatic SD1 became the last British car to win European Car of the Year. Ultimately let down by its build quality, it is affectionately known to some as 'the last Rover'. I have no idea who owns the company now – ironically, it might be Land Rover.

ROVER 2000 AIR CONDITIONING

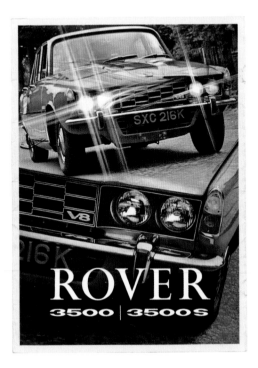

ROVER
3500 | 3500 S

ROVER

SAAB 95

SAAB

Saab AB (Svenska Aeroplan Aktiebolaget, aka the Swedish Aeroplane Corporation) was established in 1937 to build planes for the Swedish Air Force. The car-manufacturing project was started in 1945 as the company looked to diversify into new markets after the war. Their first vehicle was the Saab 92 (following on from the Saab 91 trainer aeroplane) in 1949. Improved and sequentially numbered car models followed. In 1969 they successfully merged with Scania and the millionth Saab car rolled off the production line in 1976. The iconic Saab 900 arrived in 1978, replacing the already successful 99. The rest of the Saab story is rather sad: GM came along and bought half the company, messed it up a bit by reducing the style and manufacturing quality, and by 2000 owned it all. The business became even more of a shambles, and now Saabs aren't made anymore.

Saab – a fine car for everyday use – with a charm all of its own, and high-ly individual technical qualities. A prestige car, with many Saab owners who boast often and boast willingly about their car. It is a pleasant family car with a personal style of its own – and with sporty features if you want it that way. Drive it! Just feel how well it holds the road! How safe it is!

SAAB manufactures both aeroplanes and cars—they began by making aeroplanes and then took up cars. It is not easy to imagine a better background for car manufacture than advanced aeronautical technology. In the case of the Saab car, it has signified a great deal for the shapes, the speeds, and everything which influences quality and safety. By the way, have you ever heard about Draken (The Dragon)? It's not the name of one of Saab's car models—it's one of the world's best supersonic jet fighters, designed and built by SAAB.

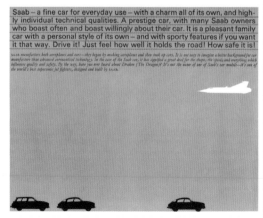

SIMCA 1000

SIMCA

The company name is an acronym of Société Industrielle de Mécanique et Carrosserie Automobile, which roughly translates as the Society for Mechanical and Car Body Parts. Started by Fiat in 1934, the company was increasingly involved with Ford Europe and eventually fell under the control of Chrysler in 1970. Chysler also bought the Rootes Group, forming Chrysler Europe. There were a few successful Simca models, the last being the Chrysler SImca 1307, which was known in the UK as the Chrysler Alpine.

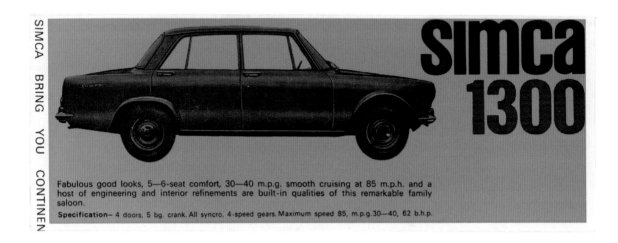

SIMCA BRING YOU CONTINEN

simca 1300

Fabulous good looks, 5—6-seat comfort, 30—40 m.p.g. smooth cruising at 85 m.p.h. and a host of engineering and interior refinements are built-in qualities of this remarkable family saloon.

Specification— 4 doors, 5 bg. crank. All syncro, 4-speed gears. Maximum speed 85, m.p.g. 30—40, 62 b.h.p.

SIMCA 1301
SIMCA 1501

simca 1000

SIMCA 1000

SKODA

The Czech car manufacturer began as bicycle-maker Laurin & Klement in 1895, moving into motorbikes and finally cars by 1905. In 1925 they were acquired by Skoda Works, an expanding arms manufacturer. Absorbed into the communist planned economy in 1948, by the 1980s their successful but dated rear-engine cars were ubiquitous and the butt of endless jokes, more than likely due to their communist origins. After the Velvet Revolution, Skoda partnered with Volkswagen and the comedy reputation has slowly diminished. The company could not escape the VW emissions testing scandal of 2015, when it was found that 1.2 million Skoda cars had been fitted with emissions-cheating software. The origins of the winged-arrow logo remain a mystery.

New SUNBEAM rapier H120

SUNBEAM **ROOTES**

SUNBEAM

The Staffordshire-based bicycle company dates from 1888, with car production starting in 1901. Success with motor racing, land-speed records and aero-engine manufacture could not prevent mounting debts and the company was absorbed by the Rootes brothers in 1934. Rootes combined Sunbeam with Clement Talbot to create Sunbeam Talbot, the idea being to build quality cars at competitive prices.

In 1953 the Sunbeam Alpine arrived and the Talbot name was dropped. A collaboration with Carroll Shelby (racing driver and god of engine modification) gave rise to the Sunbeam Tiger, which went on to sell 3,000 units. By 1964, 30 per cent of Sunbeam was in Chrysler's hands – and chaos reigned going forward. The last car bearing a Sunbeam badge was produced in 1978.

The new look of things to come from TOYOTA, Japan's No. 1 Automobile Manufacturer

TOYOTA

An inventive loom manufacturer, Sakichi Toyoda started Toyoda cars in 1933 as a division of his Toyoda loom works. The name was changed in 1937, following a public competition to design a new logo. Toyoda means 'fertile rice paddy', which is a little old fashioned for a car company, so Toyota was chosen, which also takes eight brush strokes to write in Japanese, and eight is a lucky number. Several of the company's vehicle names from the 1940s and 1950s are still in use: the Corona, the Crown and the 1966 Corolla have become the best-selling nameplates in the world, surpassing 44 million sales.

TOYOTA ♔ CROWN
2600 Automatic Hard Top

TOYOTA CARINA
1600 De Luxe Saloon

How much does your car rely on you?

TRIUMPH HERALD 1200 AND 12/50 SERIES

TRIUMPH

Starting life as a bicycle company in Coventry in 1897, Triumph motorcycles began in 1902. A large British army commission in WWI made Triumph Britain's biggest motorbike manufacturer. After buying the Dawson Car Company in 1921, car-making flourished and the business was renamed the Triumph Motor Company in 1930. Following financial difficulties the motorbike and bicycle divisions were sold off, but in 1939 the Triumph Motor Company went into receivership. In 1944 what was left of the business was bought by the Standard Motor Company, with the intention of building competitive sports saloons. Early important cars are the Triumph Roadster and the Triumph Renown, both stylish cars built using army-surplus aluminum. The famous TR range began in 1953 with the introduction of the TR2 (the TRX and TR1 only reached prototype stage). Standard Triumph was bought by Leyland in 1960, merging with British Motor Holdings to become British Leyland in 1968. Luckily Triumph had employed the design talents of Giovanni Michelotti from the late 1950s: the string of classic vehicles he created included the Herald, Dolomite, Spitfire and Stag. But by the late 1970s the Triumph brand was flagging, with the only new vehicle on the scene the rather Marmite TR7. By 1984 the Triumph name had disappeared.

Triumph put in what the others leave out

TRIUMPH69

Triumph 1500 TC

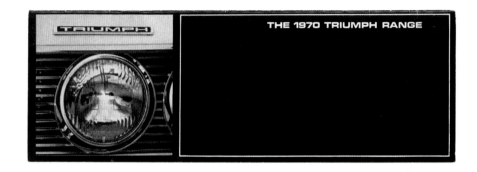

THE 1970 TRIUMPH RANGE

TRIUMPH VITESSE

THE SMOOTH SIX

STANDARD TRIUMPH
A member of the Leyland Motors Group

TRIUMPH HERALD 1200 & 12/50 SERIES

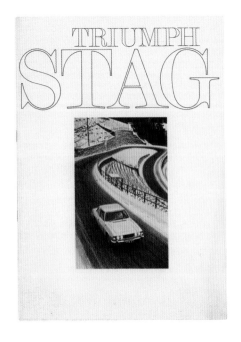

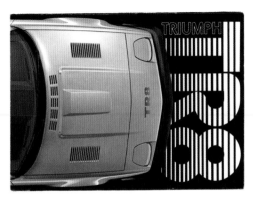

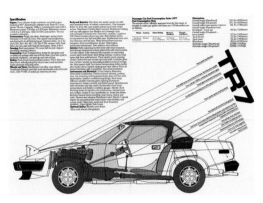

"So smooth is the flow of power, so cushioned the effect of the turbo, that what little time is lost in gearchanging is minimal, the sensation being of a jet swooping towards flight down a runway."
Motor

Turbo TVR

TVR
goes hatchback!

TAIMAR

TVR

Engineer Trevor Wilkinson established Trevcar Motors in 1946 to carry out general maintenance jobs. The name was gradually changed (with letters dropping out) to TVR Engineering. In 1949 the company built its first chassis, followed by a short series of hand-built, bespoke racing cars culminating in the TVR Sports Saloon, a sporty kit car, released in 1954. Chassis manufacturing increased, with their first cars, the Coupe and Open Sports, originating in the late 1950s – but only running to a handful of units. The first 'major' production model was the Grantura, followed by the Griffith. However, the company was dogged by problems. Poor distribution, production and reliability along with a lack of racing success forced them into liquidation in 1965. TVR were revived by two shareholders, and the brand struggled on with poorly received new models. Only at the 1970 Earls Court Motor Show, when model Helen Jones was hired to pose naked on the TVR stand (astride a TVR Vixen), did the company finally receive some badly needed attention. The following year TVR employed two topless models (Helen Jones and Susan Shaw), getting double the response. After this it all gets a little dull, with underperforming cars and factory conflicts. Eventually a Russian banker bought the company, split it up and resold it. TVR still exist, but are heavily in debt to the Welsh government.

VIXEN 1600

VAUXHALL

Originally founded in Vauxhall by Alexander Wilson in 1857 as a marine-engine manufacturer, the company became Vauxhall Iron Works by 1897, with the first car being built in 1903. Named Vauxhall Motors in 1907, after some pre-war racing success the company was acquired by General Motors in 1925. Expansion followed, but factory production turned to the Churchill tank during WWII. Several popular models were produced after the war, including the classic Victor, but these were slightly hampered by poor construction, overly 'American' styling and corrosion issues. Introduced in 1963, the Viva range was to run for the next sixteen years. This was followed by the hugely successful Chevette and Cavalier, both based on Opel models. GM slowly began to consolidate Vauxhall and Opel across Europe, and the positive step of 'Opelising' Vauxhall in the UK began. Demand and build quality improved, with the Cavalier topping 130,000 sales a year. The model was finally discontinued in 1995, after twenty years. In 2017 GM sold their Vauxhall Opel subsidiaries to Group PSA. Group PSA is now part of the giant Stellantis N.V.

The new Cresta by Vauxhall

VICTOR 101

DXD 567C

It's Beautiful! New Viva Estate

Vauxhall
Viva

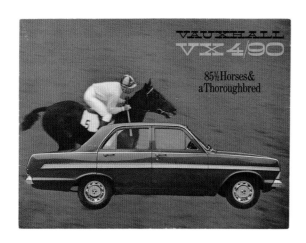

VAUXHALL
VX 4/90
85½ Horses & a Thoroughbred

five vivas for '66

Viva SL Super Luxury Saloon

1595 c.c. + 85.5 b.h.p. + 0-50 11 secs. + 90+ m.p.h.

Viva
fourdoor

Vauxhall Viva. 1256, 1800, 2300.

JET SMOOTH
WHISPER QUIET
ALL NEW **VIVA**
VAUXHALL

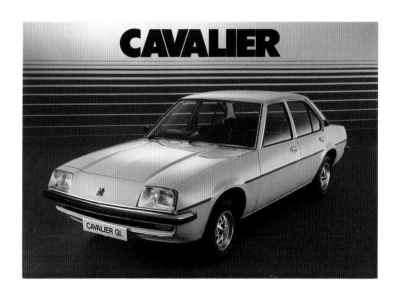

Vauxhall
Victor
Estates

VAUXHALL

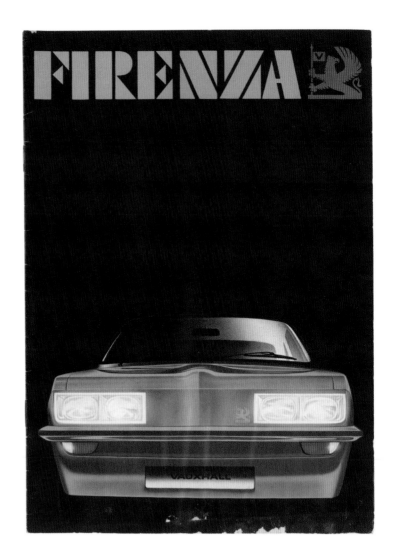

FIRENZA

VOLVO 1800S

VOLVO

The word Volvo translates from Swedish as 'I roll' – and was chosen because the company intended to make ball bearings. SKF (Svenska Kullagerfabriken) registered the subsidiary name in 1915, but ended up making cars instead. The first Volvo car – prioritising the idea of safety – rolled off the production line in 1927. Twenty years later they began to export to the American market with some success, eventually opening a factory in Canada in 1963, their first outside Sweden. Known for their safety innovations, Volvo were the first to use laminated glass as well as the patented three-point safety belt (in 1959). In 1975 the company acquired DAF and launched the big-selling 340 (based on a DAF prototype). Interestingly, the Volvo CEO at the time decided that Volvo were too small to succeed in the giant car market. They were bought by Ford in 1999.

VOLVO 1965

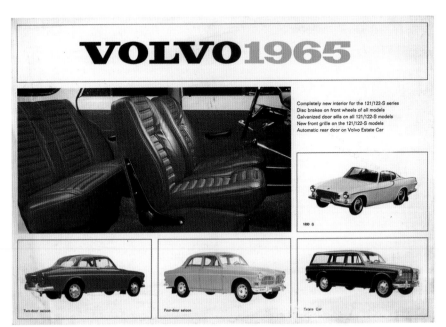

Completely new interior for the 121/122-S series
Disc brakes on front wheels of all models
Galvanized door sills on all 121/122-S models
New front grille on the 121/122-S models
Automatic rear door on Volvo Estate Car

1800 S

Two-door saloon

Four-door saloon

Estate Car

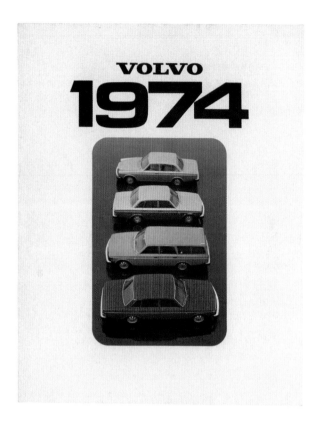

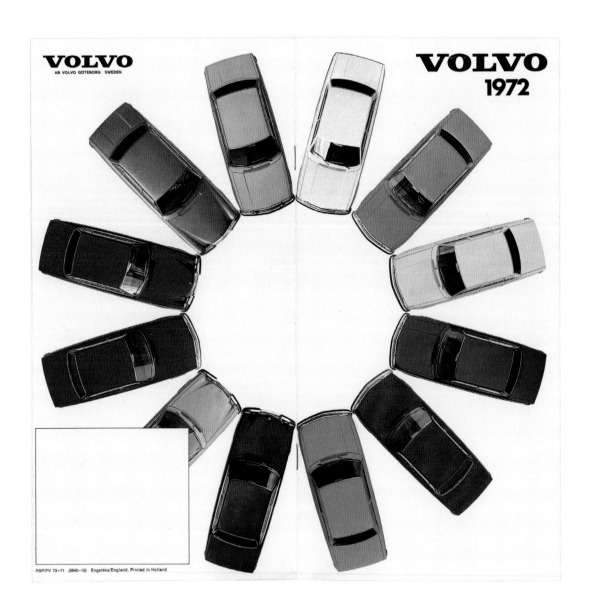

VOLVO

AB VOLVO GÖTEBORG SWEDEN

VOLVO
1972

RSP/PV 73—71 (5640—10) Engelska/England. Printed in Holland

VOLKSWAGEN

The company was founded in 1937 by the German Labour Front at the request of Adolph Hitler, who wanted a 'people's car', a small affordable vehicle for two adults and three children. The business was registered as the Company for the Preparation of the German Volkswagen Ltd. By 1938, using designs by Ferdinand Porsche, prototypes had been produced. At the outbreak of war, just a handful of finished cars had been made at the newly named KdF-Stadt factory. As the war ended, the company and factory were saved from destruction by Major Ivan Hirst of the British Army Royal Electrical and Mechanical Engineers. An experienced engineer, he was put in charge of the factory's future and made responsible for the removal of an unexploded bomb that had landed between some very valuable machinery. He soon realised that the KdF-Wagons manufactured at the factory were exactly what the British army needed. After a demonstration, the British army placed an order for 20,000.

While the order was impossible to fulfil immediately, it was the spark needed to bring the factory and its workforce back to life. During this period the factory was temporarily known as No.2 REME Auxiliary Workshop. By 1946 they could make 1,000 cars a month and the company was renamed Volkswagen, with the factory being renamed Wolfsburg. Switching to civilian production in 1947, and using the simple 'one model' policy (i.e. making just the Type 1), Volkswagen became a symbol of German regeneration and the Type 1 car quickly gained the nickname of the 'Käfer' (Beetle). The rest is history we all know, including those classic adverts, 21 million units sold and one even appearing in *Sleeper* (1973). The VW range slowly expanded, and with the purchase of Auto Union and NSU the company introduced further globally successful models based on Audi designs. The Volkswagen Group is currently the largest car-maker in the world.

as a convertible and as a coupé.

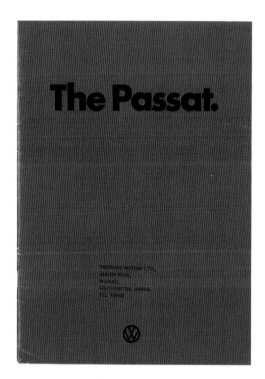

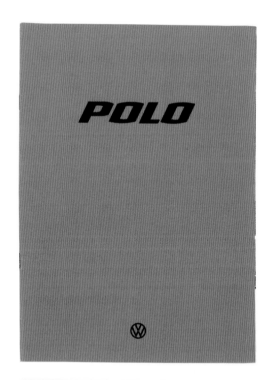

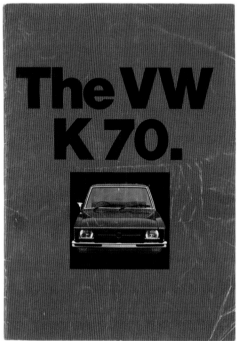

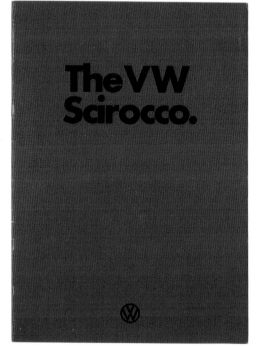

The Beetles.

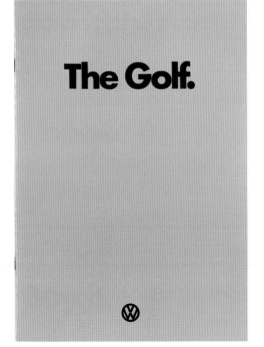

The Golf.

See it.

The Golf is a stylish new car that brings family motoring down in size. Small as it is on the outside, it's a full four seater on the inside. With a practical rear tailgate that'll handle loads of things.

Drive it.

The Golf is easy to handle and fun to drive. It has a lively water-cooled engine, a front wheel drive layout and an advanced suspension system.

Choose it.

There's a whole range of Golfs to choose from. It's available as a 3 or 5 door saloon. With an 1100 50 bhp (DIN) or a 1500 70 bhp (DIN) engine. In standard or luxurious L trim.

Own it.

With the help of your local VW dealer. He'll arrange finance for you. He'll provide insurance through VW's own insurance service. And he'll keep your Golf running smoothly with VW Computer Diagnosis.

Love it.

The Golf has a lot of endearing features. It's economical. And it requires precious little attention (10,000 miles between full services). Last but not least it's a Volkswagen, so it's good and reliable.

Buy it.

A car that makes sound sense. Sound financial sense. Sound family sense. Sound traffic sense. And sound environmental sense. This catalogue will help you make your choice.

Volkswagen

VW de Luxe Sedan

The de Luxe Sedan is not only honest and functional, but a car you'll love to drive.
New standards of Volkswagen leadership are created every year. Yet the basic design remains the same because motoring millions want it that way. Economical; robust.
Lasting in performance and value.
Tip-top road holding: air-cooled rear engine, low centre of gravity, independent wheel suspension with torsion bars, direct steering.
Low wind resistance and clear view of road almost up to bumpers.
Easy to drive and park.
Quality workmanship with four-coat finish of synthetic resin paint – garage unnecessary.

Plus cost-saving Volkswagen Service, trained mechanics and genuine VW spare parts throughout the world.
Open-car enthusiasts who do not choose the Convertible, will appreciate the de Luxe Sedan with sun-roof – simple to open and to secure in any position, even while driving.
Those for whom motoring is essentially a sun-and-air sport will choose the VW Convertible. With clean racy lines, this is a genuine convertible whose sides go right down.
With top dismantled, the elegant style is emphasized.
Fully proof against wind and weather when the top is up.
Large safety glass rear window.

VW Convertible

VW Karmann Ghia Coupé

Internationally acclaimed – a connoisseur car for people of taste.
A pure thoroughbred, racy in every line, without being an out-of-reach luxury.
A mature combination of sleek-line coachwork plus the proved VW engine and chassis.
The enduringly graceful body lines partner the elegant interior.
Broad, form-fitting seats, separately adjustable, ensure top comfort seating and relaxed driving even on long trips.
Fitted rear bench seat allows car to be used as three or four seater. No luggage problems.
The spacious compartment behind the rear seat gives double capacity when the back-rest is folded forward. More luggage goes in the generous space under the front hood.

The racy spirited car for hard-to-please motorists who enjoy open-air driving on the open road.
The centrally placed handle turns in a jiffy, and the pliant top folds automatically down, lying so flat at the rear that the car's chic contours are even further emphasized.
Graceful looks and eye-catching elegance, sure road holding and proved VW economy distinguish both Ghia models.

VW Karmann Ghia Convertible

An exciting new car.

The VW 411 LE.

With luxury car luxury.

With sports car chassis.

With rather special seats up front.

With a double-joint rear axle like the Porsche's.

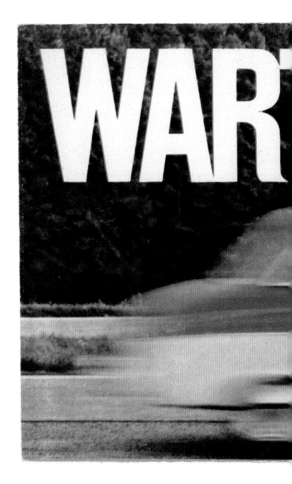

WARTBURG

This German car-maker, founded in 1898, was named after the castle that overlooks the factory. The name was dropped when the company was sold on in 1904, but revived (for the second time) in 1956. Located in the communist German Democratic Republic, it began exports to West Germany and other countries in 1960, with the popular Wartburg 353 and its variants in production from 1966 until 1988. After reunification, the small East German company could not compete with West German efficiency and closed in 1991.

TBURG 1000

THE ASHLEY LINE
FOR SPRITE I

Quickly detachable GT hardtop
Lightweight forward – hinging bonnet

No modern car enthusiast in the 1960s, 1970s or 1980s could resist dipping into the car-accessories scene. A new car stereo? Extra front and rear lights for those very dark streets? Maybe a novelty car 'fanfare' to wake up the neighbourhood? Or perhaps just a simple roof rack for when you all go on holiday – that falls off at speed on the A3, just like ours did. One 'accessory' company worth pointing out is Ashley (aka Ashley Laminates) who were independent coachbuilders making bodyshells but also bonnets and hard tops for factory-produced sports cars.

THE ASHLEY LINE

FORD ACCESSORIES

FOR YOUR NEW CORTINA

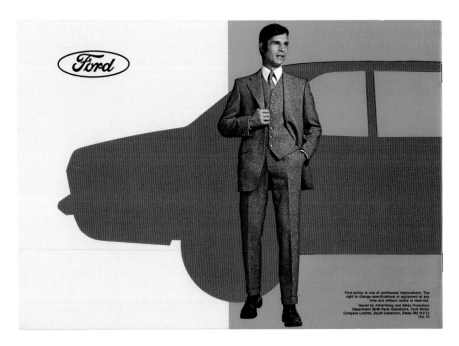

FORD ESCORT ACCESSORIES

VAUXHALL VIVA

ACCESSORIES

The '79 Vauxhall Viva is a car you'll be proud to own – and you'll want to personalise it with high-quality Vauxhall Approved Accessories. These, plus In-Car Entertainment equipment and Car Care aids, are all available from your nearest Vauxhall dealer.

VAUXHALL CHEVETTE

ACCESSORIES

The '79 Vauxhall Chevette is a car you'll be proud to own – and you'll want to personalise it with high-quality Vauxhall Approved Accessories. These, plus In-Car Entertainment equipment and Car Care aids, are all available from your nearest Vauxhall dealer.

Approved Accessories for the New Viva

The car that takes a lot of beating.

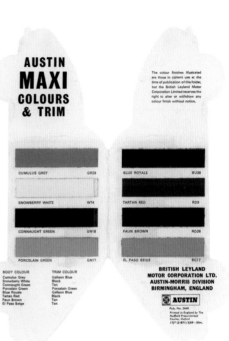

AUSTIN MAXI COLOURS & TRIM

The colour finishes illustrated are those in current use at the time of publication of this folder, but the British Leyland Motor Corporation Limited reserves the right to alter or withdraw any colour finish without notice.

CUMULUS GREY	GR29	BLUE ROYALE	BU38
SNOWBERRY WHITE	WT4	TARTAN RED	RD9
CONNAUGHT GREEN	GN18	FAUN BROWN	RD26
PORCELAIN GREEN	GN17	EL PASO BEIGE	BG17

BODY COLOUR	TRIM COLOUR
Cumulus Grey	Galleon Blue
Snowberry White	Black
Connaught Green	Tan
Porcelain Green	Porcelain Green
Blue Royale	Galleon Blue
Tartan Red	Black
Faun Brown	Tan
El Paso Beige	Tan

BRITISH LEYLAND MOTOR CORPORATION LTD. AUSTIN-MORRIS DIVISION BIRMINGHAM, ENGLAND

AUSTIN

Pub. No. 2640
Printed in England by The Nuffield Press Limited Cowley, Oxford
17/7 (21871) 5/69—50m.

Lots of car companies squeeze colour and trim options into the final pages of their standard car brochures. But dig a bit deeper and you can find some surprisingly well-designed colour keys for whole ranges, single models and even pamphlets with unexpected swatches of fabric attached. Of course, there is always a chance of coming across an unusual colour name – Fjord Blue (Ford, of course), Cavalry Fawn (Vauxhall), 7845 (Skoda) or Bedouin (British Leyland). These names only really come into their own today – if you buy a classic car from a collector, they will always quote you the correct colour name.

Ford
Colour
Guide

PASSENGER CAR
COLOUR GUIDE

FROM FORD OF BRITAIN

COLOUR
SELECTOR

AUGUST, 1978

Ford Colour & Trim Guide

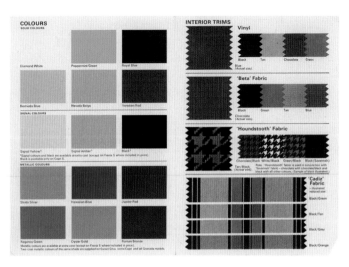

FARBKARTE · COLOR CHART · CARTE DE NUANCES · TAVOLA COLORI

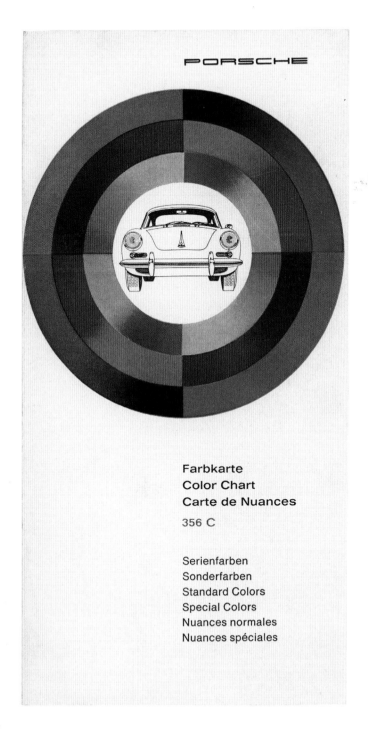

PORSCHE

Farbkarte
Color Chart
Carte de Nuances

356 C

Serienfarben
Sonderfarben
Standard Colors
Special Colors
Nuances normales
Nuances spéciales

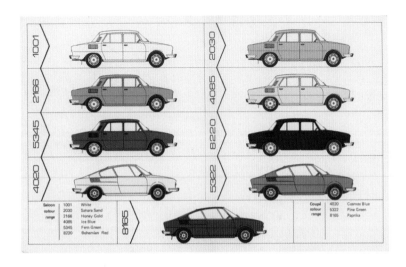

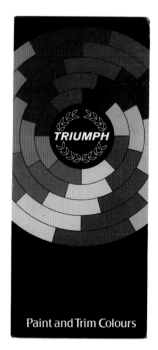

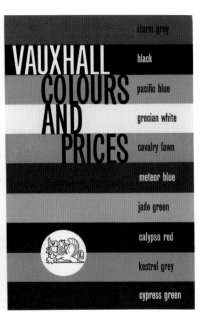

VAUXHALL COLOURS

Two-Tone VICTOR Estate Cars

- kestrel grey
- storm grey
- calypso red
- grecian white
- jade green
- cypress green
- pacific blue
- meteor blue

VAUXHALL COLOURS AND PRICES

- storm grey
- black
- pacific blue
- grecian white
- cavalry fawn
- meteor blue
- jade green
- calypso red
- kestrel grey
- cypress green

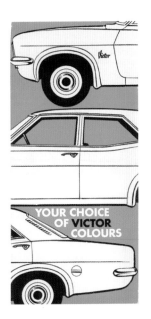

YOUR CHOICE OF VICTOR COLOURS

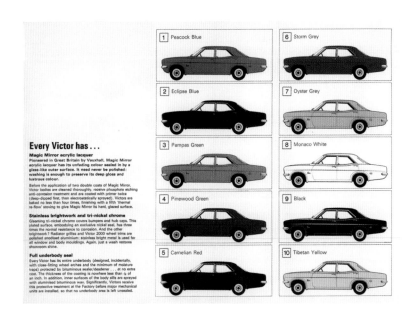

Every Victor has . . .

Magic Mirror acrylic lacquer
Pioneered in Great Britain by Vauxhall, Magic Mirror acrylic lacquer has its unfading colour sealed in by a glass-like outer surface. It need never be polished: washing is enough to preserve its deep gloss and lustrous colour.

Before the application of two double coats of Magic Mirror, Victor bodies are cleaned thoroughly, receive phosphate etching anti-corrosion treatment and are coated with primer twice (deep-dipped first, then electrostatically sprayed). Victors are baked no less than four times, finishing with a fifth 'thermal re-flow' stoving to give Magic Mirror its hard, glazed surface.

Stainless brightwork and tri-nickel chrome
Gleaming tri-nickel chrome covers bumpers and hub caps. This plated surface, embodying an exclusive nickel seal, has three times the normal resistance to corrosion. And the other brightwork? Radiator grilles and Victor 2000 wheel trims are polished anodised aluminium: stainless bright metal is used for all window and body mouldings. Again, just a wash restores showroom shine.

Full underbody seal
Every Victor has its entire underbody (designed, incidentally, with close-fitting wheel arches and the minimum of moisture traps) protected by bituminous sealer/deadener . . . at no extra cost. The thickness of the coating is nowhere less than 1/16 of an inch. In addition, inner surfaces of the body sills are sprayed with aluminised bituminous wax. Significantly, Victors receive this protective treatment at the Factory before major mechanical units are installed, so that no underbody area is left unsealed.

1 Peacock Blue	6 Storm Grey
2 Eclipse Blue	7 Oyster Grey
3 Pampas Green	8 Monaco White
4 Pinewood Green	9 Black
5 Carnelian Red	10 Tibetan Yellow

VOLVO

1980
COLOUR
AND
UPHOLSTERY

1973 Volkswagen

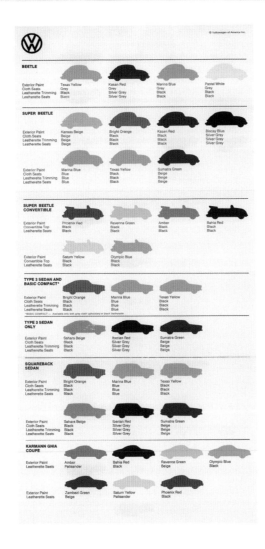

As handsome as they are practical

BEDFORD

DORMOBILE

caravans for '66

I find brochures for vans and commercial vehicles difficult to ignore, as they form an integral part of my nostalgic vision of transport. Who can forget the burglar vans in *The Sweeney* (always Commers) or the bashed-up converted Transit for sound-system transportation in the classic 1980 Brixton-based film *Babylon*. There's also the escapist dream that is the camper van – a VW, a Devon, a Westfalia. You can't drive into Cornwall these days without bumping into most of the population of vintage classic campers, now seen as the ultimate surfing accessory. My wife has always wanted a VW Camper – but I can't surf. And I can't afford one either.

OCT 1971.

four berth
moto-caravan

THE
CANTERBURY
SEEKER

CANTERBURY INDUSTRIAL PRODUCTS (AVELEY) LTD.
CHERRYDOWN · BASILDON · ESSEX
Telephone BASILDON 23458 Cables CANTACAR

A MEMBER OF THE BUDGE BROTHERS GROUP OF COMPANIES

When you open up the Commer SPACE Van

Commer | 15 cwt. to 3 ton models

You're in for a big surprise

We
Give you
The Earth

Ford Transit based Motor Caravans

The Ford Transit Formula

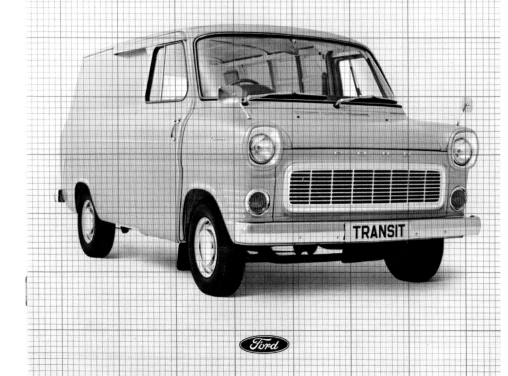

Ford Transit
A Ford of Britain Product. *Ford*

Long Wheelbase Van
25, 30 and 35 cwt payloads.
2 litre 85.5 bhp V-4 petrol
engine.
4-speed all-synchromesh
gearbox.
Diaphragm clutch.
Diesel optional on 25 cwt
model (and 30 and 35 cwt
for limited application).

"You get nearly truck
carrying capacity with 2 litre
economy, and that's quite
a combination. Enough
power? You just try to catch
one of my Transits when
it's in a hurry!"

"The Transit doesn't seem
to feel the bumps. And she
doesn't roll so much on
corners either."

"Oh yes, much the best
van I've ever driven. Wish
my car was as good . . ."

". . . Lots of blind corners
and quite a few steep hills.
The Transit's an excellent
van under these conditions,
you know, and as handy
as you could ask for . . ."

"I bet you fellows at Ford
never thought a Transit
would be used for this!"

SUBARU 360
TRUCK
FLAT-BED
TRUCK
VAN

DEVON MOTOR CARAVANS

Thank you to the following people who backed this book:

Aaron Rice
Adam Dineen
Adam Humphries
Adam Orton
Adam Warwick Hall
Adam Wheway
Adrian Smith
Adrian Turner
Adrian Zak
Aiden Naughton
Alan Beeson
Alasdair Cirrigal
Alex Jennings
Alex Moresby
Alexander and Callum
Alexander Neumann
Alfonso Ambles
Alister Babb
Andrew Burke
Andrew Nicholas
Andrew Perks
Andrew Preshous
Andrew Rutland
Andrew Schilling
Andrew Symington
Andy Carter
Andy Essex
Andy Holloway
Andy Morten &
Jon Mills from Shindig
Andy Via
B G Brand
B Yates
Barry Sowle
Ben
Ben Hayes
Ben Johnson
Ben Lind
Ben Reed
Ben Richardson
Ben Scott
Berlinster /
    Michael Anhalt
Blizz
Bob Fischer

Bob Jaroc
Bob Stanley
Brooks Moses
C Hathway
Carl Moss
Cesar Carrocera
Chap Godbey
Chaz Scholefield
Chris Allen
Chris Cameron
Chris Herbert
Chris Lee
Chris Mawson
Chris Sherlock
Chris Wilderspin
Chris Woods
Clay Gardiner
Colin Andrews
Colon Morris
Courteney Ferris
Craig Leggat
Daddy Bones
Dale Everett
Dan Williams
Dannovision
Darren Stephens
Dave High
Dave Mitchell
David Clayforth
David Evans
David Goodge
David Hasler
David Jefferies
David Morison
David Nulty
David Tatlow
David Ward
David Warley
Davis Clynch
Demetrius Romeo
Denis O'Brien
Derek Collie
Derek Ham
Derek Mantle
Dice Industries

Didier Deridder
Doug Keeley
Douglas Green
Eamonn Murphy
Elliott Elliott
Emanuele Orru
Eric Horstman
Exit
Frances Castle
Fraser Bensted
Fred Deakin
Gareth Rimmer
Gary Baker
Gary Davison
Gary Fairhead
Gary Godwin
Gary Lester
Gary Northfield
Gary Tompkins
Gaz Payne
Geoff Stone
Glenn Law
Glyn Bush
Glyn Roberts
Graeme lilico
Gray Brown
Greg carey
Groovy DJ Anne
Frankenstein
Hazel Palmer
Herb Hemenway
Hesham Sabry
Hugh Wheelan
Iain Gray
Ian Green
Ian Lambe
Ian Quann
Ian Warner
Ian Yates
Jake Morrison
James Dawes
James Hyman
James Little
James McNally
James Newport

James Postlethwaite
James Wright
Jamie Thompson
Janathan Sharp
Jane Farrell
Jared taylor
Jason Capper
Jason Draper
Jason Garrattley
Jason Hazeley
Jason Jackson
Jeff Smith
Jez Morewood
Jim Hunt
Jo A
Jodie Wood
Joe Orr
Johan Ramm
John Clarke
John Field
John Harman
John Stapleton
Johnny Dodgem
Johnny Horth
Jolyon
Jon Hobs
Jonathan Carr
Jonathan L Howard
Jonny 7
Josh
Julian Benton
Justin Merritt
Justyn de Looze
Karen Atherley
Karin Kross Levenstein
Karina Townsend
Kerrin Mansfield
Kevin Younger
Kimberley Bright
Lance Lawton
Larry Loggins
Lawrence Staden
Lee Abrahams
Lee Henderson
Liz Hutchinson

Lol Lambert
Lorenzo Dutto
Lucien Smith
Lyle Owerko
M. Fitzpatrick Murphy
Maike Palma
Make Cassella
Malcolm Goldie
Marc Jones
Marc Rouleau
Marcell Nagy
Marcus hearn
Maria Kikillos
Mark Box
Mark Colwill
Mark Hynds
Mark Reed
Mark Riley
Martin Bainbridge
Martin E Stein &
  Scott A Saxon
Martin Kearney
Martin Lovegrove
Martin Walsh
Martyn Duckmanton
Matt Blandford
Matt Button
Matt Mead
Matt Rooke
Matt Simpson
Matt Skinner
Matthew Barraclough
Matthew Fletcher
Matthew Norman
Max Clemens
Max Leonard
Michael Cummings
Michael Hampton
Michael Keeley
Michael Reeves
Michele Marietta
Mick Crawford
Misser gra
Mister Joel
Morgan Williams

Nathan Thomas
Ned Bintcliffe
Neil Johnson-
  Symington
Neil McFarland
Neil Mortimer
Neill Child
Nicholas Stewart
Nick Frost
Nick Hindle
Nick Stone
Nigel Hunt
Nigel Proktor
Nik Nak Stocks
Oli van der Vijver
Olivier Ducret
Owain Perry
Patrick Dibben
Paul Bines
Paul Binning
Paul Bowe
Paul Callanan
Paul Kelly
Paul Putner
Paul Tiffen
Paul Wain
Paul Weller
Paul Wilson
Perryn Edwards
Pete brand
Pete Chrisp
Pete Owen
Peter Aldridge
Peter Hart
Peter Leahy
Peter Pollard
Peter Vamos
Phil Baker
Phil Clarkson
Philip Clarkson
Philip Gorman
Philip Lacey
Post Utility
R J Salusbury
Rachel Bird

Rebecca Warren
Reuben Willmott
Richard Boud
Richard Hughes
Richard Jones
Richard Mayston
Richard Pennington
Richard Rackham
Rob Cornish
Rob Preuss
Rob Price
Rob Schofield
Robert Hutchison
Robert Kirkup
Robert Sinclair
Robert Wells
Robert Yates
Rory Johstone
Rpbert Krajewski
Ruffles
Rune Christiansen
Sam Harkham
Sam Whatmore
Sarah Measday-Ralls
Scott William Hall
Sean Phillips
Shaun Fowler
Shaun Reynolds
Simon Barnett
Simon Blackmore
Simon Clarke
Simon Davis
Simon Harper
Simon Hayman
Simon Holmes
Simon Jones
Simon Josebury
Simon McLean
Simon Webb
Simon Zaccagni
Skywayler Hammar
Slag Andrzejczak
Stephan Work
Stephen Cranham
Stephen Currie

Stephen James Kelly
Stephen Leighton
Stephen Morris
Stephen Pain
Stephen Simms-
  Luddington
Stephen Wilkinson
Stewart Green
Stewart Hannan
Stuart Edwards
Stuart Galbraith
Stuart Jones
Stuart Parkins
Sukhdev Sandhu
Supercollider /
  Steve Potzrayner
Tanya Jones
Terrence Guerin
The Creative Fund
Thomas Patterson
Thomas Vincent-
  Townend
Tim Jones
Tim Olden
TIm Riley
Tim Wilkinson
Tom Hamid
Tony Horton
Tony Jordan
Trevor King
Ulf Pederson
Val Palmer
Valery Carpentier
Vicki Reeve
Vincent Bouvelle
Wayne McCann
Wayne Tomlinson
William Falconer
Wolfgang Buchgraber
www.45cat.com
Z Sattar

We have tried to find out who the creative folk were behind the brochures in this book, but unfortunately, it has proved impossible. There are no indications as to which studios, designers or photographers may have been responsible for the material we have featured. Whoever they may be, we thank and praise them.

First published in 2021

FUEL Design & Publishing
33 Fournier Street
London E1 6QE

fuel-design.com

Scans, research and text by Jonny Trunk
Retouching and colour balancing by Lili Martinez at Poporo Creative and Derek Collie

Edited by Jonny Trunk, Damon Murray and Stephen Sorrell

Designed by Murray & Sorrell FUEL
Printed in China

Distributed by Thames & Hudson / D. A. P.
ISBN: 978-1-9162184-4-4

Special thanks to the following amazing and generous experts and dealers who helped with the few elusive brochures I could not find:
Retro Automotive Products
(retroautomotiveproducts.com)
David Plummer
Martin Adams

Special thanks also to Fred Deakin and Lee Henshaw